THE DISASTER PLANNING HANDBOOK

FOR LIBRARIES

ALA Editions purchases fund advocacy, awareness, and accreditation programs for library professionals worldwide.

THE DISASTER PLANNING HANDBOOK

FOR LIBRARIES

Mary Grace Flaherty
with Katherine R. Greene and Michelle Runyon

ALA Editions

CHICAGO 2022

MARY GRACE FLAHERTY is professor emeritus at the School of Information & Library Science at the University of North Carolina at Chapel Hill. She is a former IMLS Fellow and Fulbright scholar. Throughout her career, Flaherty has worked in academic, medical research, special, and public libraries. She experienced disaster response and recovery firsthand when she was serving as a public library director, and the region was inundated with catastrophic flooding.

CONTRIBUTORS

Katherine R. Greene received her MSLS degree in archives and records management from the University of North Carolina at Chapel Hill in 2021. Her thesis, "Catch Them If You Can: An Evaluation of Archival Security Practices in New England," studied New England repositories' adherence to security best practices to protect their collections from theft.

Michelle Runyon received their MSLS degree in archives and records management from the University of North Carolina at Chapel Hill in 2020. They have worked in various archives and records management institutions and are now the digital archivist at the College of William & Mary.

© 2022 by Mary Grace Flaherty

Extensive effort has gone into ensuring the reliability of the information in this book; however, the publisher makes no warranty, express or implied, with respect to the material contained herein.

ISBNs: 978-0-8389-3799-0 (paper); 978-0-8389-3643-6 (PDF); 978-0-8389-3814-0 (ePub)

Library of Congress Cataloging-in-Publication Data
Names: Flaherty, Mary Grace, 1960- author. | Greene, Katherine R., author. | Runyon, Michelle, author.
Title: The disaster planning handbook for libraries / Mary Grace Flaherty with Katherine R. Greene and Michelle Runyon.
Description: Chicago : ALA Editions, 2022. | Includes bibliographical references and index. | Summary: "This handbook provides an array of resources to enable library staff to serve their communities in disaster planning, response, and recovery"—Provided by publisher.
Identifiers: LCCN 2021031229 (print) | LCCN 2021031230 (ebook) | ISBN 9780838937990 (paperback) | ISBN 9780838936436 (pdf) | ISBN 9780838938140 (epub)
Subjects: LCSH: Library buildings—Safety measures—Planning. | Library materials—Conservation and restoration—Planning. | Emergency management.
Classification: LCC Z679.7 .F57 2021 (print) | LCC Z679.7 (ebook) | DDC 025.8/2—dc23
LC record available at https://lccn.loc.gov/2021031229
LC ebook record available at https://lccn.loc.gov/2021031230

Cover design by Alejandra Diaz. Composition in the Skolar Latin and Bilo typefaces.

♾ This paper meets the requirements of ANSI/NISO Z39.48-1992 (Permanence of Paper).

Printed in the United States of America
26 25 24 23 22   5 4 3 2 1

CONTENTS

ACKNOWLEDGMENTS *vii*

INTRODUCTION *ix*

CHAPTER 1	**Setting the Stage** *coauthored with Michelle Runyon*	1
CHAPTER 2	**Preparedness Is Key: Planning for Disasters** *with Katherine R. Greene and Michelle Runyon*	15
CHAPTER 3	**The Human Element**	39
CHAPTER 4	**Our Natural Environment** *with Katherine R. Greene*	63
CHAPTER 5	**Physical Facilities**	93
CHAPTER 6	**Archives and Special Collections** *by Katherine R. Greene and Michelle Runyon*	111
CHAPTER 7	**Looking Ahead: Future Opportunities**	121

APPENDIX: Model Memo of Understanding, National Library of Medicine *131*

INDEX *137*

ACKNOWLEDGMENTS

THANKS TO KATIE GREENE AND MICHELLE RUNYON, WHO ARE RESPONSIBLE FOR chapter 6 in its entirety. In addition, Katie's interviews with librarians and subsequent field reports in chapter 4 remind us that disasters have names, faces, locales, and outcomes; she also assisted with chapter 2. Michelle provided insight throughout and contributed to chapters 1 and 2. As noted in the chapters, Michelle conducted the interview with Winston Atkins in chapter 2, and the interview with Bradley Daigle and Flavia Ruffner in chapter 6.

Thanks also to our other contributors who lent their expertise: Christian Edwards, Michele Hayslett, Brenda Linares, and Emily Vardell. Thanks to the librarians who shared their disaster experiences: Miriam Andrus, Nancy Clark, Susan King, Teresa Newton, and Steven Williams. Thanks to our other interviewees, Winston Atkins, Bradley Daigle, and Flavia Ruffner.

I learned firsthand how to get through a disaster with a positive outlook from all the folks in the village of Sidney and at the Sidney Memorial Public Library in upstate New York. Though the list of ardent supporters is too long to include here, I would like to express thanks especially to coworkers Pamela Gilbert, Tamme DeMulder, Judy Ives, Marcie Gifford, and Adrienne Hendricks, board president Spike Paranya and his wife, Kathy, and the Friends of the Libraries board president, Mary Jane Gelder.

Thanks also to the folks at the Kellogg Free Library for keeping me stocked with ILL requests and curbside pickup while crafting this volume. Thanks to Louise Penny for the escape to Three Pines Village, the perfect antidote for long days of writing and thinking about disasters during a pandemic. Editor Patrick Hogan's buoyant enthusiasm and advice made for a better final product; thank you.

And as always, thanks to Les who, through his 30+ years as a humanitarian engineer-epidemiologist, has been involved in far more than his fair share of disasters, but still manages to maintain an unwavering optimism, keep the home fires burning, and offer endless and abiding support.

INTRODUCTION

> Noah's ark was the first disaster emergency response vehicle.
> —Earl Johnson

IN 1980, THE MOST EXPENSIVE AND COMPREHENSIVE STUDY OF ITS KIND EVER FUND-ed by the U.S. government to that date was published under the title The Global 2000 Report to the President (Barney 1980). Commissioned by President Jimmy Carter, it predicted that after the year 2000, climate change would be the greatest existential threat to the United States. This prediction was largely ignored for two decades, leaving many to wonder why we did not prepare and plan a little more assertively.

We live in a time when democracy is reportedly on the decline across the globe, and the U.S. intelligence community reports that for the next two decades, the gap between people's expectations and the ability of governments to fulfill them will grow both at home and abroad (Freedom House 2020; National Intelligence Council 2021).

As librarians, we work in organizations that can help to level the social playing field. The COVID-19 pandemic is yet another reminder that inequities, and the need for our services, are often magnified during and after natural and social crises. Given that both weather and socially driven crises are likely to increase in the decades to come, we should not repeat the process of failing to prepare for what is widely predicted to arise: more disasters. Yet, for librarians, this topic is far from being about gloom and doom! A large body of examples has arisen where library workers have provided spectacular and inspirational services during disasters. During disasters and emergency situations, our communities rely upon library services and support the most; and a large part of disaster planning consists of setting the stage for resilient approaches during these times.

According to the Disaster Information Management Resource Center of the U.S. National Library of Medicine, a disaster is "an occurrence such as a hurricane, tornado, storm, flood, high water, earthquake, drought, blizzard, pestilence, famine, fire, explosion, building collapse, transportation wreck, terrorist event, bioterrorist event, pandemic, power failure or other similar natural or man-made incident(s)." For as long as there have been humans (and even before that time), there have been disaster challenges in all shapes and sizes.

Over the past decades, we have witnessed stunning, escalating changes in weather-related emergencies as the climate becomes increasingly volatile, with longer storm seasons, rising tides, more frequent wildfires, and prolonged drought. Emergencies have not been limited to weather events, however. Structural and cultural inequities have culminated in social unrest and upheaval, which are part of the national landscape as well. More than any time in our history, community-building and community efforts will be vital to our survival as a species.

As information hubs and resource providers, it makes sense for libraries and library workers to be involved in community disaster preparedness, response, and recovery efforts. Most libraries provide their services without membership requirements and without charge. Whether in a university setting, urban center, or rural village, libraries serve the vital roles of information nexus and gathering centers, places where users can find support in a variety of ways. As became evident during the COVID-19 pandemic, in some communities, and disproportionately in the poorest ones, libraries are the only option for high-speed internet access. During disaster recovery and response, this access can be a lifeline; it is vital for correspondence, and for submitting recovery claims and all types of forms.

In each chapter that follows, we address different aspects of dealing with disasters. We start in chapter 1 with a summary of the U.S. historical context, and how that context has shaped disaster management approaches today. We also outline the intersection of libraries with disaster response. In chapter 2 we discuss disaster planning, including conducting risk assessments, and we provide some ideas for program opportunities. Chapter 3 is dedicated to the human element in disasters, and describes the stages communities go through before, during, and after a disastrous event. This chapter also covers individual responses and ways to offer support, and touches upon trauma-informed service provision. Human-caused disasters, such as active shooters, bomb threats, civil unrest, arson, and the COVID-19 pandemic, are discussed here as well.

According to the National Weather Service, 98 percent of all presidentially declared disasters in the United States are weather related, so it is no surprise that the longest chapter in this book, chapter 4, is dedicated to natural disasters. In this chapter we have included various field reports from librarians across the United States who have shepherded their communities through an emergency situation, and come through the other side. Their experiences provide context and hope, and reiterate how important it is to plan for the unexpected. Because libraries are usually located in physical structures, chapter 5 is dedicated to the caretaking of facilities, and provides checklists and templates for the building considerations to include in a disaster plan. Chapter 6 considers disaster preparedness in special libraries and archives, and chapter 7 provides fodder for future consideration and action, such as information literacy during disaster response, and roles for librarians in disaster preparedness and training.

As advocated in chapter 3, risk assessments are a natural part of the disaster planning process. To determine what subjects to include in this volume, we considered the most likely risks or disaster challenges a typical library in the United States might encounter. Thus, there are some subjects that have received less coverage than others, such as technological security challenges. While a breach in computer security or a ransomware attack can certainly be disastrous, this is a threat that will rapidly change shape and form, and is usually addressed on an organizational level by the information technology department. The responsibility for dealing with such challenges will often differ dramatically between organizations, so these types of security challenges fall more firmly in the specific domains of information technology and cybersecurity, and as such they are larger subjects to consider in and of themselves, and fall outside the purview of this volume. The tools we have included for crafting a disaster preparedness plan (e.g., the fema.gov website) do include resources and guidance on ensuring computer security, however.

Although the most consequential man-made disaster, war, has given us some of our most inspiring examples of librarians serving their communities, such as the chief librarian in Basra, Alia Baker, who saved 30,000 books from destruction during the Iraq War (Dewan 2003), a consideration of this topic is beyond the scope of this volume. And because so much of disaster preparedness, response, and recovery is supported by local, regional, and national institutions, this book has a heavy slant toward the U.S. experience.

Throughout this volume there are suggestions for tools, activities, and easy-to-adapt templates. Our hope is that no matter where your library or organization is in the disaster planning cycle, this book will make the process a bit less daunting and maybe even a bit enjoyable (see, for instance, the disaster board games in chapter 3 to kick things off).

Though disasters test us in unforeseen and unexpected ways, there are some bright spots to consider. For instance, the COVID-19 pandemic has taught us all sorts of lessons and has engendered numerous learning opportunities, such as better time management and priority-setting, increased self-sufficiency, and the mastery of new skills. In libraries across the United States and the globe, we have discovered and integrated new and innovative ways to offer resources and services. Even disasters can have silver linings.

On a final note for this introduction, during every presidential election cycle since I turned eighteen I received a postcard from my father (as long as he was alive), admonishing me to *Hope for the best, prepare for the worst.* (He appended *VOTE* to the adage.) It was not until I was in the midst of responding to record flooding as a public library director that I realized I have carried this advice throughout my professional life, and it is the perfect summary for disaster planning. My hope is that this book will help to make the planning and preparation processes smoother, and play some small role in helping to build more resilient libraries and communities.

REFERENCES

Barney, Gerald O. 1980. *The Global 2000 Report to the President—Entering the Twenty-First Century: The Technical Report.* Washington, DC: U.S. Government Printing Office.

Dewan, Shaila K. 2003. "After the War: The Librarian." *New York Times*, July 27. www.nytimes.com/2003/07/27/world/after-the-war-the-librarian-books-spirited-to-safety-before-iraq-library-fire.html.

Freedom House. 2020. "New Report: Freedom in the World 2020 Finds Established Democracies Are on the Decline." https://freedomhouse.org/article/new-report-freedom-world-2020-finds-established-democracies-are-decline.

Johnson, Earl. 2020. *Finding Comfort during Hard Times: A Guide to Healing after Disaster, Violence, and Other Community Trauma.* Lanham, MD: Rowman & Littlefield.

National Intelligence Council (U.S.). 2021. *Global Trends 2040: A More Contested World.* Washington, DC: U.S. Government Printing Office. www.dni.gov/files/ODNI/documents/assessments/GlobalTrends_2040.pdf.

National Library of Medicine, Disaster Information Management Resource Center. 2021. https://disasterinfo.nlm.nih.gov/.

National Weather Service. 2021. "NWS StormReady Program." www.weather.gov/stormready/.

CHAPTER 1

Setting the Stage

Experience is a hard teacher; she gives the test first, the lesson afterward.

—*Vernon Law*

DISASTERS, IN THEIR MANY VARIATIONS AND POSSIBILITIES, ARE AN INTEGRAL ELE-ment of our shared human experience. Across the globe, we are struggling with the effects of the COVID-19 pandemic, a stark reminder of our human and organizational interconnectedness. As described by Oliver-Smith (1998), there's mutuality between nature and culture; and while disasters are positioned in both our social and material spaces, they also exist in a space created by these intersections. Hence, to understand disasters, our approach should take into consideration the "web of relations that link society (the organization and relations among individual groups), environment (the network or linkages with the physical world in which people and groups are both constituting and constituted) and culture (the values, norms, beliefs, attitudes, knowledge that pertain to the organization and those relations)" (Oliver-Smith 1998, 186). While the aim of this chapter is not to discuss theoretical approaches to the understanding or study of disasters or the history of disaster response in the United States, it is important to recognize the complicated history and effects of disasters as our world becomes increasingly interconnected and complex.

This chapter continues with a discussion of historical precedents and legislation that have paved the way for the current emergency management landscape in the United States, and introduces the intersection of libraries and disaster management.

The Role of the Federal Government

In the United States, the first example of the federal government's involvement in local disaster relief occurred in 1803, when a congressional act was passed to provide assistance to the town of Portsmouth, New Hampshire; the town had been devastated when fire ravaged it, and many businesses and homes were destroyed. The act temporarily suspended the "collection of bonds due by merchants . . . who have suffered by the late conflagration of that town" (New England Historical Society n.d.). The path forward from that time has been bumpy and entangled, in terms of legislation and support for disaster assistance. A century and half later, when Congress passed a nationwide disaster policy in 1950, there were already more than 128 different laws pertaining to disaster response on the books (Bittle 2020).

The history of disaster management in the United States has been built upon the integral involvement of the federal government, a seemingly haphazard process in which libraries had little to no involvement. In the 1930s, the Bureau of Public Roads and the Reconstruction Finance Corporation were given authority to make loans available for the reconstruction and repair of public facilities after disasters. During this same period, the Tennessee Valley Authority was created by congressional charter for electricity generation, flood control, and forest regeneration; and the Flood Control Act was passed. The act afforded more authority for the U.S. Army Corps of Engineers to design and construct flood control projects (Federal Emergency Management Agency, or FEMA, 2014).

The 1950s have been characterized as the Cold War era, with an increased emphasis on civil defense. The Federal Civil Defense Administration (FCDA) was created, and many communities had a civil defense director. These directors have been described as the "first recognized face of emergency management in the U.S." (FEMA 2014, 2). In 1958, the FCDA was merged with the Office of Defense Mobilization (whose mission was to mobilize resources in case of war) to form the Office of Civil and Defense Mobilization.

With the 1960s came a number of major natural disasters (the Hebgen Lake earthquake in Montana, Hurricane Donna in Florida, Hurricane Carla in Texas). At this time, the newly installed Kennedy administration shifted gears with regard to emergency management and disaster response. President Kennedy created the Office of Emergency Planning within the White House to address natural disasters, while civil defense remained situated within the Department of Defense.

As the 1960s progressed, there were more earthquakes and hurricanes across the country. The pattern of passage of ad hoc legislation for disaster relief funds continued. However, when it became apparent that flood protection was cost-prohibitive and was not included in homeowners' insurance policies, this prompted the passage of the Flood Insurance Act of 1968, which created the National Flood Insurance Program (FEMA 2014).

By the 1970s, there were at least five federal departments and agencies involved in emergency management, and "when one looked at the broad range of risks and potential disasters, it became apparent that more than 100 Federal agencies were involved in some aspect of risk and disaster management" (FEMA 2014, 4). This fragmented response indicates that at this time federal emergency management was not a high priority (Mener 2007), and the same fractured pattern permeated the state and local levels as well. The lack of a unified federal response agency led to calls by the National Governors Association for reform, and during this push the accident at the Three Mile Island nuclear power plant occurred, prompting further attention to the matter (FEMA 2014). Thus, in 1978 President Carter provided a plan that would consolidate efforts and establish an overarching federal agency for emergency management response, mitigation, and preparedness. Accordingly, the Federal Emergency Management Agency (FEMA) was created in 1978–79, with its director reporting directly to the president.

The establishment of FEMA did not remove the burden of disaster response from state and local agencies, however; federal monetary and logistical resources were meant to augment, not substitute for, local resources (Miskel 2006). For most disasters, the system of local governmental response, which leverages private-sector organizations, along with state and federal support, has worked well. Large and small private and nongovernmental organizations, such as the American Red Cross and the Salvation Army, faith-based organizations, and private individuals, have played a major role in supporting communities during disasters. Local and state governments have been and remain the central logistical support mechanism, however; they also provide support personnel through departments such as fire and police and emergency services. States can also call upon the National Guard for additional support as needed. State governors can request aid, relief, and reinforcement from the federal government when all local and state resources have been overwhelmed or exhausted. The governor's request is reviewed by FEMA, and if approved, the next step is certification by the president. Once the president certifies that a major disaster has occurred, FEMA becomes involved and a "federal coordinating officer" is appointed to oversee all federal assistance in the designated area affected by the disaster. But though the federal government has sometimes been called in to provide coordination and personnel in disaster regions, for the most part, federal support has been secondary and has come in the form of post-facto financial reimbursements (Schneider 1995).

In the early and mid-1980s there just weren't many major natural disasters, so FEMA's directors placed the emphasis on national security issues, rather than on natural disaster preparedness (FEMA 2014). But when it became apparent that natural disasters could have devastating consequences, and that preparedness efforts should reflect this reality, Congress passed a major reform of federal disaster policy. In the midst of this reform, though, the "promise of FEMA and its ability to support a national emergency management system remained in doubt" (FEMA 2014, 6). In the late 1980s and early 1990s, a series of natural disasters (e.g., Hurricanes Andrew, Hugo, and Iniki, and the Loma Prieta earthquake) further demonstrated that FEMA's response capability was limited.

New leadership was installed at the agency in the early 1990s, with the first director hired who had actual emergency management experience, James Lee Witt. Under Witt's direction, the agency became more streamlined and was able to respond effectively to a number of consequential disasters, while its efforts expanded to include mitigation efforts before disasters strike.

With the Oklahoma City bombing in 1995, FEMA folded addressing terrorism into its purview, a trajectory that gained momentum after the 9/11 attacks in 2001. With the appointment of Joe Allbaugh as FEMA director by President George W. Bush, the Office of National Preparedness was re-created with a new mission, which was to focus on terrorism response. In 2002 the Homeland Security Act was signed into law; this was a major governmental reorganization that created the Department of Homeland Security. The act consolidated 22 different federal agencies (including FEMA) with 170,000 employees into a single new department with a cabinet-level secretary (Kettl 2004). The intent was to streamline interdepartmental cooperation and improve national security.

Throughout these decades, libraries of all types were still largely viewed as mere materials repositories. While they may have provided a range of services and programs, their chief role was to provide access to and storage for books and other print materials. During crises, the emphasis was on protecting the libraries' collections and providing general information to the public. Libraries' role as community service hubs was not yet fully recognized or exploited at this time.

When Hurricane Katrina hit Louisiana in 2005, it became apparent that the unwieldy, highly bureaucratic Department of Homeland Security was not the model of interagency cooperation and communication that had been envisioned when it was created. The federal government's response to Hurricane Katrina was beset by failures, including the fact that there was no adequate process or system for providing rapid, accurate damage assessment (Mener 2007). While state and local authorities were (and are) charged with providing these assessments, there was no backup mechanism in place for providing the information when those authorities were completely overwhelmed.

Figure 1.1 shows the timeline of major federal involvement in disaster relief in the United States from 1803 to 2005, beginning with the Portsmouth, NH, flood and ending with Hurricane Katrina. We chose to end with 2005 and Hurricane Katrina because the catastrophic consequences of that event served as a national wake-up call for all organizations and institutions with regard to emergency preparedness. However, at that same time FEMA explicitly stated that "libraries are not essential services" (National Library of Medicine 2019), and thus failed to recognize the role that libraries could play in disaster response and recovery.

The history of governmental involvement in emergency management has been a complicated and complex one. As stated earlier, most disaster preparedness and response activities occur at the local and state levels. And though the federal government's involvement in the response and recovery process has not always been ideal, in extreme circumstances (of which we are seeing more and more) it does provide significant support.

1803 PORTSMOUTH FIRE — Congress passes Act Local disaster relief

1930s AUTHORITY TO GIVE LOANS GRANTED — Bureau of Public Roads; Reconstruction Finance Corp.

1934 FLOOD CONTROL ACT

1950s CIVIL DEFENSE — Cold War Era

1961 OFFICE OF EMERGENCY PREPAREDNESS — Created by JFK

1968 FLOOD INSURANCE ACT

1974 DISASTER RELIEF ACT

1978 FEMA CREATED — Initiated by Carter in 1978

1995 OK CITY BOMBING — Domestic Terrorism

2001 9/11 ATTACKS — International Terrorism

2003 DHS CREATED — Initiated By GW Bush in 2002

2005 HURRICANE KATRINA "DEBACLE" — Category 5

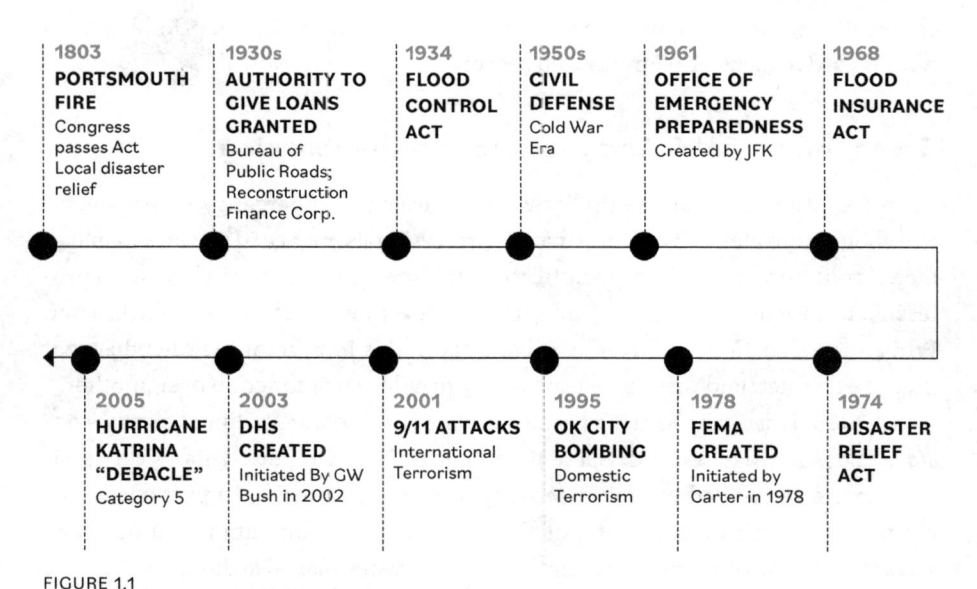

FIGURE 1.1
Abbreviated timeline of U.S. federal involvement in emergency management from 1803 to 2005
Source: Based on FEMA's "Introduction to Emergency Management"

For libraries, this history has several implications. The federal government's response mechanisms, which were very fragmented in the last century, were consolidated in 1979 under the newly created Federal Emergency Management Agency, which in turn has been re-formed with a very broad mandate, ranging from natural disasters to disease outbreaks to terrorist attacks. Because FEMA is a bureaucracy that provides expertise and funds rather than an organization with access to water pumps and sandbags, it tends to provide financial aid after the response to a disaster, for repairs of existing damage and improvements that will mitigate future risks.

As discussed in more detail in the chapters that follow, the reimbursement process implies the need for meticulous record-keeping of costs and activities during and after a crisis. This is due in large part to the nature of the bureaucratic procedures in the wake of a disaster; the disbursal of recovery funds will be assessed by individuals far removed from the crisis, and often months later. In contrast, funds from the county and from local philanthropies and organizations will probably be awarded because individuals will have witnessed the disaster and appreciated what the organization went through, and how it functioned before the crisis. This chapter continues with an overview of the role of libraries in the United States with regard to disaster planning and response.

Recent History: U.S. Libraries and Disaster Planning

To understand the relationship between libraries and emergency management, one should consider (1) how information professionals engage in disaster management for library and archival facilities and holdings, and (2) how information professionals support the broader community's recovery in the aftermath of a disaster. While these functions can overlap substantially, it is important to remember that they are distinct, and certain measures may privilege one function over another.

In 2005, Hurricane Katrina became a major flash point for libraries to reconsider their approaches to disaster planning. In New Orleans, Tulane University's libraries struggled with disaster response during Katrina, in part due to the limited communication capacity of the university; this limitation had not been accounted for prior to the crisis. The libraries' disaster plan also did not anticipate that emergency services across the entire city would be compromised (Corrigan 2008). The library holdings in the basement of Tulane's Howard-Tilton Memorial Library sustained significant water damage. Moreover, the library staff were not able to view and assess the damage until several days after the storm hit Tulane's campus (Topper 2011). Since that time, some libraries have taken measures to delineate multiple lines of communication in their disaster plans in order to minimize struggling with the same difficulties. While Tulane did receive FEMA funding to restore its library facilities, the university still had to pursue other funding sources to support the remodeling and reconstruction of those facilities damaged in the hurricane. These financial struggles in the wake of Hurricanes Katrina and Rita (which also occurred in 2005) had various long-term impacts for the Howard-Tilton Memorial Library and other libraries of all types in the New Orleans area (Diamond 2006; Topper 2011).

The Robert T. Stafford Disaster Relief and Emergency Assistance Act (PL 100-707, signed into law November 23, 1988; amending the Disaster Relief Act of 1974, PL 93-288) delineates the federal government's response to natural disasters. Under the Stafford Act, the U.S. president may issue federal disaster declarations; these declarations open up potential federal funding and aid for states and local governments that are responding to a given disaster. As described earlier, the governor of the state, or states, affected by the disaster must request that the president issue a federal disaster declaration (FEMA 2011). The Stafford Act was originally enacted into law in 1988, with amendments since then. Under Section 403 of the Stafford Act, FEMA may "provide Federal assistance to meet immediate threats to life and property resulting from a crisis" (FEMA 2019, 30).

In January 2011, the Stafford Act was amended to state that libraries fulfill an "essential community function" (FEMA 2019). Thus, they are eligible for temporary relocation and other federal disaster benefits. This designation—an "essential community function"—remains both practically and symbolically important because it recognizes the vital role that libraries can play in disaster response and recovery, and thus signified a major shift in philosophy over the six-year period from 2005 to 2011. According to the National Library of Medicine (2019), the following steps led to the resultant amended Stafford Act:

1. Individuals who were affected by disasters flocked to unaffected public libraries for help.
2. Librarians in states affected by Hurricanes Katrina and Rita reacted negatively to FEMA's denial of "temporary facilities" status for libraries.
3. The chief officers of state library agencies, the American Library Association (ALA), many librarians, and their supporters worked for changes to the Stafford Act.
4. U.S. Senator Jack Reed worked on behalf of libraries.

So, while civil defense directors may have been the "face" of emergency response in the 1950s, now that recognition may go to local library directors as well.

In 2017, Hurricane Maria became another point at which cultural heritage professionals reevaluated their disaster planning and response. Widespread lack of power and access to clean water across Puerto Rico made recovery for the island's libraries incredibly challenging (Davila Gonzalez 2018). The ALA partnered with REFORMA to create the Adopt a Library Program, which matched donors with libraries in Puerto Rico and the U.S. Virgin Islands that had suffered severe damage from Hurricane Maria (Tobin 2018). The ALA had previously created an Adopt a Library Program to support libraries damaged during Hurricane Katrina (American Library Association n.d.).

Intersection of Libraries and Disaster Planning

Libraries, within their organization, school, town, city, or state, interact with disaster planning processes in two ways. First, it should be clear within the library itself, and in the larger sectors such as the town or city, what is required to protect the library's assets during a disaster. Secondly, the role that the library will play for the community during a disaster should also be determined. If the library's primary role at that time is to provide internet access for the public, this will necessitate a specific series of actions and measures. If the library's primary role is to provide an emergency organizational center through the use of its meeting rooms, or to provide a tornado shelter in its basement, these call for a different planning and response process.

Building both formal and informal relationships with emergency personnel ahead of time can lead to smoother responses during a disaster and a faster turnaround time when the library can begin offering its services again. In a 2018 assessment, the New England region of the National Network of Libraries of Medicine (NNLM) found that 60 percent of respondents did have existing relationships with local emergency responders or other similar community partners (Carnes 2018). Cross-trainings between emergency responders and information professionals can foster these ties organically. Working with community partners is discussed further in subsequent chapters.

The National Library of Medicine (NLM) is a primary resource and has been in the forefront of disaster planning for U.S. libraries. Though the website was suspended in April 2020, the NLM's Disaster Information Management Research

Center (DIMRC) still has resources for the general public, emergency responders, and information professionals to use in all stages in the disaster management cycle. The NLM has also developed a variety of tools to aid in disaster response, such as mobile apps (discussed in chapter 2) and a template for a Memorandum of Understanding that is provided at the end of this book, in the appendix.

Memoranda of Understanding (MOUs) can be an effective way for libraries to mutually support one another and for government entities to commit to providing mutual aid during an emergency. Having and maintaining an active MOU with another institution can speed up response and recovery from a disaster. MOUs outline the conditions of aid, such as what material or financial support can be mutually provided, and under what conditions such aid would be made available. MOUs can be crucial under circumstances in which local, state, or federal government aid is lacking or slow to be provided. The Southeastern/Atlantic region of the NNLM endorsed a Model Memorandum of Understanding (see the "Appendix") that can guide libraries in creating their own MOUs (Brewer and Reich 2005). Keep in mind that MOUs have to follow organizational procedures and requirements. The Environmental Protection Agency Library's "Disaster Response and Continuity of Operations Procedures," for example, states that libraries which provide support to those in the EPA National Library Network through MOUs should abide by the EPA Library's Continuity of Operations procedures (Dunkin 2016).

Libraries also have access to professional networks, regional consortia, and state libraries that may serve as sources of aid and support during disaster response and recovery. The California State Library issued $200,000 in one-time grant funding to the fifteen hardest-hit local public libraries during the 2017 wildfire season (Lynch 2017). As of 2020, the Society of American Archivists offers up to $5,000 in funding to U.S. archives or special collections whose archival holdings are damaged or at risk (Society of American Archivists n.d.).

The American Institute for Conservation and Foundation for Advancement in Conservation (AIC-FAIC) offers training and consultation support to those interested in the emergency management of cultural heritage materials. Their "national heritage responders" deploy to areas affected by disasters and are available for remote consultations regarding the treatment of damaged items. These national heritage responders are conservators, archivists, and other cultural heritage professionals who are trained in how to salvage and minimize damage to cultural artifacts in the event of a natural or man-made disaster.

The Heritage Emergency National Task Force consists of fifty-eight nonprofit organizations and government entities that collaborate to support disaster management for libraries, archives, museums, and other cultural heritage institutions. The Task Force developed the Heritage Emergency and Response Training (HEART) to train emergency management professionals alongside cultural heritage professionals. These trainings not only guide how the professions should work together, but also foster bonds between local emergency responders and cultural heritage institutions (McKay 2018).

Intersection of Libraries and Disaster Response

While library workers collaborate with and support emergency responders during disaster response, they also support the general public's recovery. As organizations, libraries are well positioned for this task, given their proximal geographic location and the fact that they are generally trusted as resource providers within their communities. Libraries have often acted as information and research hubs for disaster response and as gathering places for the victims of natural disasters (Brobst, Mandel, and McClure 2012).

Internet access is a crucial feature of the services offered in libraries after a disaster, especially since many FEMA disaster assistance and some insurance claim forms are only available online now. Librarians may also help patrons and emergency responders complete insurance claims, federal or state disaster assistance forms, and other forms necessary for recovery. Librarians are instrumental in aiding patrons as they examine various options to receive disaster recovery support. The New Jersey State Library's *The Librarian's Disaster Planning and Community Resiliency Guidebook* (2013) identifies librarians as "Information 1st Responders," given the fact that they provide authoritative and truthful information to government officials, first responders, and other essential parties to help with disaster response and recovery. Now that digital resources and processes have become essential in disaster response, it is also worth highlighting the fact that librarians also support disaster recovery through their continual efforts to promote and bolster digital literacy among their patrons.

International Agencies

Though the emphasis of this chapter has been on U.S. domestic disaster management agencies, it would be remiss not to mention, albeit briefly, the multitude of international agencies involved in disaster management, including both governmental and nongovernmental organizations. Among the global agencies whose missions address emergency disaster management in some way are many United

Nations (UN) agencies, such as UNICEF (the UN Children's Fund), the UNEP (UN Environmental Programme Disasters and Conflicts sub-programme), the UNDRR (UN Office for Disaster Risk Reduction), the UNHCR (UN High Commissioner for Refugees), UN-Water, and the World Health Organization (WHO) with its regional offices, such as PAHO (Pan American Health Organization – Regional Office for the Americas of WHO). The International Committee of the Red Cross and the International Federation of the Red Cross, Direct Relief International, Medecins sans Frontieres (Doctors without Borders), and the Salvation Army are a few more examples of agencies that work in emergency situations across the globe.

This chapter has provided a brief historical overview of emergency management in the United States and laid the groundwork for a discussion of how libraries have emerged as essential partners in disaster preparedness, response, and recovery efforts.

REFERENCES

American Library Association. n.d. "Adopt a Library Program." www.ala.org/aboutala/adopt-library-program.

Bittle, Jake. 2020. "On the Waterfronts." *The Baffler* 49, no. 1.

BrainyQuote. 2021. "Vernon Law Quotes." www.brainyquote.com/authors/vernon-law-quotes.

Brewer, Michelle Volesko, and Barbara S. Reich. 2005. "Model Memorandum of Understanding for a Health Sciences, Hospital/System or Medical Library for Emergency Preparedness Support." National Network of Libraries of Medicine, Southeastern/Atlantic Region. https://nnlm.gov/sites/default/files/scr/files/mou-emergency.pdf.

Brobst, John L., Lauren H. Mandel, and Charles R. McClure. 2012. "Public Libraries and Crisis Management: Roles of Public Libraries in Hurricane/Disaster Preparedness and Response." In *Crisis Information Management*, 155–73. Cambridge, UK: Chandos.

Carnes, Sarah. 2018. "Investigating Options for Increased Awareness and Use of Disaster Preparedness, Response, and Recovery Resources among Libraries and Librarians (Part One of a Two-Part Series)." *Journal of Hospital Librarianship* 18, no. 2: 115–26. https://doi.org/10.1080/15323269.2018.1437502.

Corrigan, Andy. 2008. "Disaster: Response and Recovery at a Major Research Library in New Orleans." *Library Management* 29, no. 4/5: 293–306.

Davila Gonzalez, Geraldine. 2018. "Hurricane Maria and Its Lessons on Preservation." September 28. (Blog). *Custodia Legis: Law Librarians of Congress.* https://blogs.loc.gov.

Diamond, Tom. 2006. "The Impact of Hurricanes Katrina and Rita on Three Louisiana Academic Libraries: A Response from Library Administrators and Staff." *Library Leadership & Management* 20, no. 4: 192–200.

Dunkin, Ann. 2016. "EPA Library Disaster Response and Continuity of Operations (COOP) Procedures." Environmental Protection Agency, National Library Network.

Federal Emergency Management Agency (FEMA). 2011. "FEMA Fact Sheet: Disaster Declaration Process." www.fema.gov/pdf/media/factsheets/dad_disaster_declaration.pdf.

———. 2014. Emergency Management Institute. *Emergency and Risk Management Case Studies Textbook*. https://training.fema.gov/hiedu/aemrc/booksdownload/emoutline/.

———. 2019. "Stafford Act, as Amended, and related authorities." FEMA P-592, www.fema.gov/sites/default/files/2020-03/stafford-act_2019.pdf.

Kettl, Donald F. 2004. *The Department of Homeland Security's First Year: A Report Card*. New York: Century Foundation.

Lynch, Deborah. 2017. "California State Library Provides Aid to Libraries in Communities Hit Hard by 2017 Wildfires." California State Library. December 22. www.library.ca.gov/Content/pdf/pressreleases/WildfireLibraryFundsAwardedRelease_12_22.17.pdf.

McKay, Jim. 2018. "Public-Private Partnership Links Emergency Managers and Cultural Institutions." *Government Technology*. "Emergency Management." www.govtech.com/em/disaster/Public-Private-Partnership-Links-Emergency-Managers-and-Cultural-Institutions.html.

Mener, Andrew S. 2007. "Disaster Response in the United States of America: An Analysis of the Bureaucratic and Political History of a Failing System." *CUREJ: College Undergraduate Research Electronic Journal*. University of Pennsylvania. http://repository.upenn.edu/curej/63.

Miskel, James F. 2006. *Disaster Response and Homeland Security: What Works, What Doesn't*. Connecticut: Praeger Security International.

National Library of Medicine. 2019. Disaster Information Management Research Center. "A Seat at the Table: Working with the Disaster Workforce." www.nlm.nih.gov/dis_courses/seat_at_table/02-000.html.

New England Historical Society. n.d. "New Hampshire: The Portsmouth Fires That Turned the City to Brick." www.newenglandhistoricalsociety.com/the-portsmouth-fires-that-turned-the-city-to-brick/.

New Jersey State Library. 2013. *The Librarian's Disaster Planning and Community Resiliency Guidebook*. www.njstatelib.org/wp-content/uploads/2013/01/The-Librarian-Guidebook-July-21-Final.pdf.

Oliver-Smith, Anthony. 1998. "Global Changes and the Definition of Disaster." In *What Is a Disaster? Perspectives on the Question*, ed. E. Quarantelli, 177–94. London: Routledge.

Robert T. Stafford Disaster Relief and Emergency Assistance Act, PL 100-707; amending PL 93-288.

Schneider, Saundra K. 1995. *Flirting with Disaster: Public Management in Crisis Situations*. New York: M.E. Sharpe.

Society of American Archivists. n.d. "National Disaster Recovery Fund for Archives | Society of American Archivists." www2.archivists.org/groups/saa-foundation-board-of-directors/national-disaster-recovery-fund-for-archives.

Tennessee Valley Authority. n.d. "Our History." www.tva.com/about-tva/our-history.

Tobin, Tess. 2018. "Puerto Rico Recovery Efforts: Our Help Is Still Needed." *International Leads: A Publication of the International Relations Round Table of the American Library Association* 32, no. 1: 10–11.

Topper, Elisa F. 2011. "After Hurricane Katrina: The Tulane Recovery Project." *New Library World* 112, no. 1/2: 45–51.

CHAPTER 2

Preparedness Is Key
PLANNING FOR DISASTERS

An ounce of prevention is worth a pound of cure.
—Benjamin Franklin, 1736

WHEN BENJAMIN FRANKLIN MADE HIS TIMELESS STATEMENT, HE WAS ADMONISHING the citizens of Philadelphia to be involved in fire awareness and prevention. Almost 300 years later, his wisdom still rings true, and appears to be widely relevant in American libraries.

In a "Disaster Planning for Libraries" class, taught semi-regularly at UNC-Chapel Hill's School of Information & Library Science, one of the assignments is for graduate students to investigate a specified number of libraries and determine if they have a currently available disaster plan. The students make their own choices of library and region, and of library type. The class completes this assignment so that students have a better understanding of what disaster preparedness, plans, and planning look like from an operational standpoint.

Because this exercise was not designed to capture a systematic or randomized sample, the findings are not generalizable, but they do provide a snapshot and enable a starting point for discussing the importance of having a disaster plan in place. Invariably, the students report that some library staff are reluctant to admit they don't have a plan, many others can't locate the plan, and some libraries are part of a larger system (i.e., a county government or library system) that oversees emergency management; thus, they use the system's plan and don't have a library-specific plan for their organization. Table 2.1 reports the cumulative results of those inquiries, from four individual classes (representing a total of 32 students) offered from 2014 to 2019.

As shown in table 2.1, in the case of the public libraries that were contacted, almost half (45 percent) of the 178 total did not have a disaster plan in place; in the case of academic libraries, 85 percent did have a plan in place. In two cases,

TABLE 2.1
Number of libraries with disaster plans

Library Type	Plan - Yes	Plan - No	Total
Public	98 (55%)	80 (45%)	178
Academic	88 (85%)	15 (15%)	103
State		2	2
School		1	1
Total	186 (65%)	98 (35%)	284

students investigated state libraries and determined that they did not have a plan (or the staff whom they contacted could not determine if there was a plan, thus leading the students to conclude that operationally there's no plan for staff to consult). In one case, a student contacted a school library; he was told they had no known disaster plan. With a multitude of tools and templates readily available, and an ever-increasing incidence of disaster events, *every* library should *at the very least* have some type of rudimentary disaster and service-continuity plan in place, and ensure that library workers know where to find it.

What Do We Mean by a Disaster Plan?

For every library, the optimal disaster plan will be a little different, though all plans will primarily take into consideration the protection of people, collections, and equipment. A library disaster plan is ideally formed in response to three factors:

- What disastrous events or circumstances are most likely to occur or are of highest concern to your library?
- What are the unique circumstances or characteristics of your facility (i.e., its elevation above a floodplain, its structural integrity, high occupancy at certain times) that could lead to unacceptable outcomes that you need to mitigate?
- What are the special expectations or priority concerns of your team and community?

Thus, a tornado-oriented disaster plan might be completely different for a three-story wood-frame building than it would be for a one-story, brick-and-concrete structure in the same region. A western library where wildfires are the greatest concern may have a completely different plan if the expectation is that the library will serve as an emergency shelter for the community, rather than the goal of protecting the building and contents. No matter what the challenges are, preparedness will empower staff and help to manage the impact of disasters through available documentation, regular practice, education, and appropriate supplies. Disaster plans should also provide guidance for response and recovery.

Some elements of plans will be almost universal. Virtually all facilities need a plan to evacuate the building, or have a set of standardized steps to follow when common events occur, such as a smoke alarm going off or the electricity going out. Thus, for most libraries, creating or reviewing a plan will involve assessing risks, and reviewing the plans of other institutions. The sections that follow will provide some resources and guidance for this. Other elements, such as assessing your library's own circumstances and assessing the expectations and concerns of your community, may seem like a purely internal exploration, but these can actually be influenced and guided by the plans and past deliberations of other libraries. This chapter continues with a description of the tools and key resources available from a variety of sources, discusses high-density storage, community and personal preparedness, and concludes with a brief discussion of mitigation considerations.

Disaster Planning Tools

For creating, tweaking, and updating disaster plans, the first place to start is within your organization. As was found with the class exercise described above, many libraries rely upon the larger institution in which they are embedded (i.e., a county library system or university library system) for disaster preparedness, so they may not have a library-specific plan. The role the library will play in a disaster, given differing contingencies, and in terms of service expectations (discussed in more detail in chapter 3), should be considered during the planning phases, and included in the final plan. When it comes to creating a tailored plan, there are a number of agencies and institutions that support disaster preparedness and offer a variety of tools for individuals, organizations, and communities. The sections below by no means comprise an exhaustive list of resources, but they do point to a number of free, accessible, easy-to-use tools that can be adapted for all types of organizations and situations.

FEDERAL AGENCIES
There are many federal agencies whose mission might include some aspect of emergency preparedness and response, such as the departments of Agriculture, Defense, Energy, Health and Human Services, Homeland Security, State, Transportation, and Treasury. The Environmental Protection Agency, the National Domestic

Preparedness Office, the Nuclear Regulatory Commission, the Transportation Security Administration, and the U.S. National Response Team are also involved in providing support related to emergency management.

Here, though, we will focus on federal agencies whose primary mission is directly related to disaster preparedness and response. The most familiar and important of these is the Federal Emergency Management Agency (FEMA), an agency within the Department of Homeland Security.

FEMA's website (fema.gov) has resources ranging from webinars to worksheets for individuals, organizations, and communities to help them to become prepared. FEMA's web resource called Ready (ready.gov), as its name implies, has a ready-made protocol to follow for creating a disaster plan and building an emergency kit. The website also includes resources for a variety of community members, such as individuals with disabilities, military, seniors, and pets and animals. Its "Tools for Practitioners" include planning guides and a case-study library, as well as guidance on environmental planning and historic preservation, to mention just a few tools. In addition, FEMA has tabletop exercises, a resource library for teens, and a variety of resources for kids. FEMA's ready.gov resource is the logical place to get started with disaster planning.

The National Library of Medicine's website MedlinePlus (medlineplus.gov) is a health information service that offers links to numerous other resources. Under health topics, its "Disaster Preparation and Recovery" section provides links to reliable and authoritative resources from agencies such as the National Institutes of Health, FEMA, the Centers for Disease Control and Prevention (CDC), the Mayo Clinic, the EPA, and the Food and Drug Administration. MedlinePlus is a valuable resource for getting started with and reviewing disaster planning and preparedness.

The NLM's Disaster Information Management Research Center (DIMRC) is dedicated to improving access to health information resources and technology with regard to disasters, public health emergency preparedness, response, and recovery. The center's aim is to "connect people to quality disaster health information and foster a culture of community resiliency" (disasterinfo.nlm.nih.gov). Though the DIMRC stopped updating its website in 2020, the site still offers links to extensive resources and tools, information on all types of disasters, training programs, and resources such as apps for first responders (described in more detail below). Access to this disaster literature is now available through the CDC's website (https://emergency.cdc.gov/).

The Centers for Disease Control and Prevention's website (www.cdc.gov) has an extensive list of resources and emergency preparedness tools that cover a wide range of topics, including planning, staying healthy, special populations, disability and health emergency preparedness, making water safe, pet boarding, and so on. The site's "Emergency Preparedness" section also has guidance on natural disasters and severe weather, bioterrorism, pandemic preparedness, chemical and radiation emergencies, and how to care for children during disasters. The CDC's website is a valuable resource not only for planning, but for community members (e.g., first responders) to use as well.

STATE AND LOCAL GOVERNMENTS AND AGENCIES

State government agencies are another important resource for disaster preparedness. For public libraries, state library entities often offer guidance and support before, during, and after disasters, as was the case with the Texas State Library ahead of Hurricane Laura in August 2020. At that time the state library provided advance warning, information on hurricane safety, and on recovery resources (Hunt 2020). Given the wide variety of governance and the organizational hierarchies of different types of libraries and their settings, specific state and local agencies won't be covered extensively here. It is important to ferret out ahead of time, however, what kind of support and assistance are available at state and local levels for your specific library, and to include this information in your disaster plan.

As with state and local agencies, the library's involvement with local governments around disaster planning and response will vary a lot, depending on the library's type and setting. Some logical places to go for assistance with disaster plans and preparedness are the mayor's office (or equivalent), fire and police departments, the sanitation department, and the community planning department. That said, many of the most detailed material asset-oriented elements of a disaster plan will probably depend on local agencies. For example, if you will need a generator, a sludge pump, or propane heaters for an extreme cold emergency, local agencies will be the most likely source for these. Moreover, local players will probably be the first to respond, so identifying these agencies in advance and understanding their roles will make your library's plan more effective. For instance, if the town or institution engineer knows that you plan to provide public internet services in a disaster involving widespread power outages, but that you will require a generator to provide those services, this will probably allow them to plan for, and reserve, your generator needs. If you know that your town's emergency plan involves using the local volunteer fire department as an emergency medical facility, this will allow your library to dispense vital information should such an emergency arise. Coordinating your plan with state or federal authorities does not make sense for most libraries, but coordinating your plan with local partners can have a profound effect on the success of those plans in the event they do need to be activated.

COMMUNITY AND NONPROFIT AGENCIES

The American Red Cross has long been recognized for its work in the realm of disaster relief. It responds to an emergency approximately every eight minutes, or more than 60,000 every year; 95 percent of its relief workers are volunteers, and 90 percent of the disasters they respond to are home fires (redcross.org). Besides offering a wide range of training opportunities, the Red Cross also has resources for disaster planning and preparedness, such as its three-step plan, with templates in English and Spanish, guidance for building a survival kit, and its free downloadable emergency app.

Many service organizations, such as Rotary International and Lions Club International, offer emergency assistance for disaster relief, even though they may not offer direct support for disaster planning. In addition, their local meetings may offer a forum for interacting with the greater community around disaster preparedness.

LIBRARIES THAT HAVE EXPERIENCED DISASTERS

Another valuable resource for learning about disaster plans is to examine how libraries that have been through a disaster dealt with the challenges. There are many reports in the library literature about how libraries coped with and transcended all types of disasters. Common to many of these reports are easy-to-implement tips such as an updated communication and disaster plan, good housekeeping and maintenance, keeping entryways clear, routine fire extinguisher checks, regular staff updates, practice, and drills.

SERVICE CONTINUITY PLAN

Whether you have a detailed and well-defined disaster plan in place or not, a one-page service continuity plan that can be shared with both library staff and emergency responders can prove to be invaluable. An easy-to-use template can aid with this process. The Pocket Response Plan (PReP), a tool created by the Council of State Archivists (CoSA), can be easily customized for your organization. The only requirement is that if you do use the template, attribution to the CoSA should be noted. The plan can be found at www.statearchivists.org/programs/emergency-preparedness/emergency-preparedness-resources/pocket-response-plantm-prep-tm-english-template/.

Helpful Technologies

Various technologies can aid with disaster management; and in particular, implementing mobile applications or other technologies ahead of a disaster can facilitate response and recovery. While we discuss some specific mobile apps or similar resources, it is important to evaluate for yourself what technologies will be most useful for you and your organization. The specific technologies discussed in the sections below may become obsolete over time, so we will also discuss principles and functionalities to consider when selecting resources.

When evaluating technologies to use in planning and response, one should consider if an app requires internet access to function or if some features can't be used without internet/data access. Power and internet access can be intermittent or unavailable in many disasters, so this should be taken into account before adopting a new technology for disaster management and communication.

EMERGENCY ALERTS

There are a variety of emergency alerts available for keeping informed and up-to-date. FEMA offers helpful guidelines and resources in this regard (see ready.gov/alerts). It helps to have designated staff members, such as members of the emergency management team, to receive and pass along emergency alerts for your geographic area, including notifications about natural or man-made disasters.

MOBILE APPLICATIONS

The NLM's DIMRC has developed a number of mobile applications for various smartphone platforms that can facilitate all stages of the disaster management cycle, both for librarians and emergency responders. One such tool is the Wireless Information System for Emergency Responders (WISER; wiser.nlm.nih.gov), which is intended for use by emergency responders/receivers to identify hazardous materials and treat injuries from exposure to them, as well as provide containment and suppression information.

The Chemical Hazards Emergency Medical Management (CHEMM) tool, which was formerly a stand-alone application, is now embedded into WISER and helps to identify chemical threats to health and safety. CHEMM was created for first responders and receivers, planners, and health care providers to help them plan for, respond to, recover from, and mitigate the effects of mass-casualty incidents that involve chemicals. CHEMM provides a user-friendly, comprehensive, web-based resource, and like WISER, it can be downloaded in advance, in case of an internet outage (chemm.nlm.nih.gov).

Radiation Emergency Medical Management (REMM; remm.nlm.gov) is a free database that offers various tools that can be used to identify and treat injuries from nuclear or radiological incidents. You should consider offering training workshops on these tools if such a disaster is a risk in your setting (e.g., there are 95 nuclear power plants presently in the United States, and approximately 80 storage facilities; McMahon 2019), and if emergency responders in your area aren't currently using them. All of the resources have helpful tutorials, which could be easily adapted for training purposes. This could also be an easy, low-cost way to offer library programming that would bring first responders into the library.

TRACKING TECHNOLOGIES
In some emergency situations, library staff should be able to track damaged materials. This is most likely accomplished by having a barcode-scanning mobile application, which can store and track barcodes that you scan with a mobile device. Your institution may also be able to leverage its existing tracking system for library materials. Whichever method you choose, take into account whether the system can track individual library items with a unique identifier, and the physical location of individual library materials. It may be useful to have the ability to group materials based on their format or the extent of the damage done to them; this can help when triaging damaged items and prioritizing interventions.

SOCIAL MEDIA
It is vital to practice good information literacy when evaluating news about an emerging disaster. While reputable sources may report different facts as information becomes available over time, other sources may spread misinformation, either unintentionally or intentionally. Shaping your disaster response around misinformation can slow or hinder that response. To avoid the unintentional spread of misinformation, first, follow the guidance of trustworthy sources such as local emergency management departments or other government agencies. These can include FEMA, the National Weather Service, and the National Oceanic and Atmospheric Administration, to name a few. The CDC has a digital media toolkit called "Take Action" (www.cdc.gov/prepyourhealth/toolkits/takeaction.htm) that provides guidance on natural disasters, disease outbreaks, and other emergencies. The toolkit includes social media messages and graphics, and links to additional resources.

Organizations should have procedures in place for using social media during emergency procedures, such as determining ahead of time who can post to institutional social media accounts and when they should do so. This will streamline communication to the public about disaster response and/or access to library services. This process can be facilitated by creating or adapting a social media policy that outlines employees' behavior. Figure 2.1 provides a sample social media policy, provided by the DIMRC in its course called "Social Media Analysis during Disasters."

FIGURE 2.1
Sample social media policy

INSTRUCTIONS: This sample social media policy can be adapted for use by your own organization. Once tailored to your organization, consider having employees sign or otherwise indicate agreement in relation to employees' personal use of social media.

POLICY
This policy provides guidance for employee use of social media representing [Agency], which should be broadly understood for purposes of this policy to include blogs, wikis, microblogs, message boards, chat rooms, electronic newsletters, online forums, social networking sites, and other sites and services that permit users to share information with others in a contemporaneous manner.

PROCEDURES
The following principles apply to professional use of social media on behalf of [Agency] as well as personal use of social media when referencing [Agency].

- Employees need to know and adhere to the [Agency's Code of Conduct, Employee Handbook, and other company policies] when using social media in reference to [Agency].
- Employees should be aware of the effect their actions may have on their images, as well as [Agency's] image. The information that employees post or publish may be public information for a long time.
- Employees should be aware that [Agency] may observe content and information made available by employees through social media. Employees should use their best judgment in posting material that is neither inappropriate nor harmful to [Agency], its employees, or customers.
- Although not an exclusive list, some specific examples of prohibited social media conduct include posting commentary, content, or images that are defamatory, pornographic, proprietary, harassing, libelous, or that can create a hostile work environment.
- Employees are not to publish, post or release any information that is considered confidential or not public. If there are questions about what is considered confidential, employees should check with the Human Resources Department and/or supervisor.
- Social media networks, blogs and other types of online content sometimes generate press and media attention or legal questions. Employees should refer these inquiries to authorized [Agency] spokespersons.
- If employees encounter a situation while using social media that threatens to

become antagonistic, employees should disengage from the dialogue in a polite manner and seek the advice of a supervisor.
- Employees should get appropriate permission before referring to or posting images of current or former employees, members, vendors or suppliers. Additionally, employees should get appropriate permission to use a third party's copyrights, copyrighted material, trademarks, service marks or other intellectual property.
- Social media use shouldn't interfere with employee's primary responsibilities at [Agency]. [Agency's] IT systems are to be used for business purposes only. When using [Agency's] IT systems, use of social media for business purposes is allowed (ex: Facebook, Twitter, [Agency] blogs), but personal use of social media networks or personal blogging of online content is discouraged and may result in disciplinary action.
- Subject to applicable law, after-hours online activity that violates [the Agency's Code of Conduct] or any other company policy may subject an employee to disciplinary action or termination.
- If employees publish content after-hours that involves work or subjects associated with [Agency], a disclaimer should be used, such as this: "The postings on this site are my own and may not represent my employer's positions, strategies or opinions."
- It is highly recommended that employees keep [Agency] related social media accounts separate from personal accounts, if practical.

HIGH-DENSITY STORAGE

High-density storage, a system for concentrating physical library assets in less space, is an emerging concern for disaster management in libraries. The following interview with Winston Atkins is included to illuminate how to approach disaster planning for a high-density storage facility.

Interview with Duke University's Preservation Officer

INTERVIEW BY M. RUNYON

Winston Atkins was the preservation officer at Duke University from March 2000 until his retirement in May 2020. Prior to that he was the preservation officer at North Carolina State University, and he received his MLIS degree from the University of North Carolina at Chapel Hill. During his tenure at Duke University, Atkins initiated the first disaster plan for the university's Library Service Center, a high-bay storage facility for library materials. Duke University also leases space in the Library Service Center to various nearby institutions. The following narrative was compiled after conducting an interview with Atkins.

ONE MAJOR REASON why Duke University decided to develop a disaster plan for the Library Service Center (LSC), its high-bay storage facility for library materials, is that the scope of a potential disaster in the LSC far exceeded that of a potential disaster in one of the "regular" library facilities on the Duke campus. In April 2015, there were almost 5,000,000 individual items in the LSC. The shelving density of the LSC is approximately 110 volumes per square foot of assignable floor space. By comparison, the Perkins/Bostock libraries at Duke have approximately 4.6 volumes per square foot of assignable floor space. Using testing conducted by the University of Illinois at Urbana-Champaign's Conservation Department in their own high-density storage facility (Teper 2011), Atkins and his colleagues at Duke estimated that as many as 30,000 items per sprinkler head would be damaged if the sprinklers in the LSC were triggered. Disaster recovery on this magnitude far exceeded what Duke's staff could handle in-house; the internal response team could only respond to disasters affecting 1,000 volumes or less, and this meant that Duke had to contract with an outside vendor to provide adequate support for response and recovery.

When seeking out a vendor to support disaster management for the LSC, the Duke staff encountered some unforeseen complications. For one, there were only a handful of vendors with national reputations for disaster response and recovery in libraries; this limited Duke's options when they issued a request for proposals for LSC disaster management services. In the vendor selection process, Atkins and others at Duke had expected that vendors would have conservators and other library professionals on call who could be part of the LSC's response. They discovered that this seemed not to be the case, highlighting how specialized disaster response in libraries continues to be. The Duke team began working with one vendor intensely with the expectation that the vendor would be intimately involved in the disaster planning process, so that the firm could figure out ahead of time what personnel and equipment they would need to have on hand to execute the disaster plan. Duke also wanted the vendor to understand how they fit into the complex chain of command that the university was creating for LSC response. However, this initial vendor could not provide the level of commitment to the planning process that Duke was looking for, so they eventually contracted with a second vendor to support the LSC's disaster response.

Internally, many more departments and senior staff became involved in the LSC's disaster planning process than for creating previous disaster plans. The Rubenstein Library, which houses various archives and special collections at Duke, became a stakeholder because it stores the majority of its holdings in the LSC. The Rubenstein's holdings include materials in a variety of text and non-text formats. This great variety of formats in the LSC's holdings presented additional challenges in the disaster planning process. Many library and university-level stakeholders became involved in the project as the planning became more involved. Internal stakeholders at Duke included, but weren't limited to, the Library Executive Group, Conservation Services, the Environmental Safety Office, the Risk Management Department, the

Facilities Management Department, and the Security and Facilities Department. The Facilities Management Department in particular played a key role in coordinating fire suppression or response for the LSC.

Atkins recommends beginning to create a disaster plan as soon as possible, even when the first module is constructed. The complexities and scale involved in disaster management for high-bay storage facilities necessitate early and thorough planning. Institutions should not count on their current disaster plans for other library facilities to adequately encapsulate disaster management for high-bay storage. The institution's stakeholders should be expanded in a way that is commensurate with the scale and interconnectivity inherent in the high-bay storage facility. While Atkins thought that Duke's experience with smaller-scale disasters aided some aspects of creating the LSC's disaster plan, he basically felt that the experience of creating a high-bay storage plan was very new and lacked many previous models to consult.

To strengthen the cohesion of the disaster team, Atkins further recommends using or creating a tabletop exercise to simulate response in a high-bay storage unit. This has many potential benefits, including getting staff to use the same vocabulary and understand their roles in the response effort. Each participant will bring their own approaches and vocabulary to their response strategy. The tabletop exercise allows participants to strategize how to fluidly communicate with one another and execute their roles more effectively outside of a high-pressure, active disaster. During a tabletop exercise, the participants may also realize they need to include more departments or personnel than had previously been considered. Duke itself worked on developing a tabletop exercise that simulated what would happen if there was a water leak inside the LSC.

The key takeaway from Atkins is: begin disaster planning for your high-density storage facilities as soon as possible. There will be a number of challenges that arise with the process, seen and unforeseen. However, the challenges do not become easier over time. As high-bay storage becomes increasingly commonplace in libraries, it is critical to ensure that the valuable assets contained within them are safeguarded.

Preparedness

As engaged community members, libraries of all types are strategically positioned to help their communities with disaster preparedness. They offer resources, connectivity, and access to information, and often serve as community meeting spaces. Supportive relationships cannot be contrived during a disaster event, however; they are built up over time with thoughtful, intentional, and inclusive decision-making and policies. Several of the examples presented throughout this book highlight the value of community support, in the form of financial contributions, volunteers, book donors, and the like, which can only happen when the library is a primary stakeholder and an engaged community partner. Moreover, physical and tangible forms of assistance have not always been found to be the most meaningful resource for librarians who have had to cope with disasters; often, emotional support and understanding from an invested community have been just as important in terms of providing reassurance during the recovery process. For a community to support its library in these ways, the library must demonstrate its commitment and investment in them first.

Building a relationship with local first responders is a great way to recognize the vital work they do and to familiarize them with the library at the same time. Even seemingly mundane tasks such as conducting tours of the library building, sharing floor plans, taking advantage of fire safety checks, and consulting on emergency equipment purchases (fire suppression or alarm systems, for example) can help streamline disaster response. Having a preexisting rapport can be an enormous help when only first responders are allowed in the building and library staff are not. If it is possible to evacuate materials, it is important that emergency officials know which materials to target for removal first, as discussed in chapter 5 under salvage priorities. Learning about library collections gradually in normal circumstances and feeling comfortable enough to ask staff about their priorities during the crisis itself can save valuable time and allow for more items to be saved or salvaged.

There are various local and national opportunities for information professionals to cross-train with emergency responders. FEMA offers such opportunities through its Emergency Management Institute. Some training is available online for free and counts toward various certification programs under certain conditions. The Medical Library Association's Disaster Information Specialization is a training program that incorporates coursework from FEMA, the National Library of Medicine, and the MLA itself. The program's curriculum is designed to teach information professionals or others involved in emergency management how to use their information skills to aid disaster management for libraries and the general public. FEMA's Emergency Management Institute also offers many online, independent study courses such as "Fundamentals of Emergency Management" and "Workplace Security Awareness." These courses can be taken at your own pace. There are also in-person training sessions at a FEMA site.

No matter how perfect and updated a disaster plan may be, it is of no practical use if staff are not aware of it, or they can't access or understand it. The regular inclusion of disaster preparedness "practice," with activities and training at staff meetings at all levels of the organization, can help ensure that everyone has the basic knowledge needed to navigate during a crisis. The American Red Cross offers a variety of training opportunities, such as first aid and CPR, that will help empower staff to act in an emergency situation. One library has its staff members do a monthly check of fire extinguishers on a rotating basis; this not only ensures that the extinguishers are functional and up-to-date, but the staff also acquire direct knowledge and are reminded of their locations throughout the facility regularly.

Building a go-bag—a portable kit containing the items needed for three days' survival upon being evacuated after a disaster—could be an easy starting point or activity for discussing personal emergency preparedness with library staff and community members, as described next.

---------- **What's in Your Go-Bag?** ----------

PERSONAL PREPAREDNESS IS as important as organizational preparedness. Because there are many unexpected circumstances that might require immediate evacuation, from a gas leak in an apartment building to impending flooding, it's always a good idea, if possible, to have an emergency kit with basic essentials at hand in your home. Some folks use a plastic tote bag that fits in a closet or under the bed, while others prefer an old suitcase or duffel bag. The food and other supplies in a go-bag should last an entire family, including pets, three days.

You should consider hosting a library program to solicit input from community members on their requirements in emergency situations. In the event the library becomes an emergency shelter, this information could help inform how the organization prepares. You could then follow up the discussion with an opportunity to build go-bags. Invite local businesses and organizations to participate; for instance, perhaps the bank would provide canvas bags, the local dentist offices could donate toothbrushes and sample toothpaste; and local clinics might be able to donate bandages. If the library has a Friends group, or the school has a parents' group, they might be able to provide the funds to purchase essential items as well.

The list below includes items that are generally recommended for inclusion in a go-bag; however, it should be noted that for some households the investment may not be within their financial means. If possible, the library should consider coordinating having go-bags available that could be used for community members in need.

ESSENTIALS
- Water and food
    - » one gallon of water per person for three days
    - » water purification tablets
- Nonperishable food items that do not require cooking or water
    - » protein bars

OTHER NECESSITIES
- First aid kit
    - » a minimal one includes: adhesive tape, elastic wrap bandages, assorted bandage strips, liquid bandage, rubber tourniquet, antiseptic wipes, antibiotic ointment, gauze pads, acetaminophen and ibuprofen, tweezers, scissors, instant cold packs, blanket, thermometer, first aid manual
- Flashlight
    - » remove batteries until needed to avoid corrosion
    - » extra batteries
- Plates, utensils, can opener, a few tools
    - » consider a Swiss Army knife: different variations have utensils, screwdrivers, can openers, and so on
- Matches (in waterproof container)
- Whistle
- Tape, plastic sheeting
- Have some cash on hand if possible, in smaller bills
    - » if there is no power, ATMs and credit/debit cards will not work

PERSONAL NEEDS
- Eyeglasses, contact lens solution
- Hygiene supplies (including toilet paper, toothbrush, etc.)
- Over-the-counter and prescription medications
    - » if you cannot pack the medications, use a note to remind yourself to take them with you
- Any supplies for children (e.g., diapers)
- Clothes as needed
    - » including hats, sturdy shoes

PAPERWORK
- Copies of birth certificates, IDs, medical cards, insurance policies, account information, and prescriptions, or save encrypted copies or photos of these on a secure online mechanism

- Passport, Social Security card
    » these may not necessarily belong in your go-bag as a regular practice, but should be retrieved in case of evacuation
- Printed list of phone contacts
    » in case it is not possible to use the phone

OTHER CONSIDERATIONS
- Establish a contact point
    » an out-of-town relative or friend as contact for everyone in the family, to relay updates and messages
- A deck of cards, or favorite (small) game, especially if there are children
- Make a list of items that you might use too regularly to store in the kit, for example, prescription sunglasses, cash, diapers

---

As COVID-19 has taught us all too well, beyond the go-bag, it pays to prepare for disasters and other unexpected situations (e.g., power outages; toilet paper shortages) that require sheltering in place. Items that might be helpful to regularly have on hand include candles, a generator, extra toilet paper, canned goods, and a can opener.

Risk Assessment

Conducting a risk assessment is an integral component of disaster planning because it ensures the consideration of issues specific to your organization, such as the likelihood of specific weather events in your region. Given that it is virtually impossible to prepare for every possibility when it comes to emergencies, risk assessment tools can help identify and codify likely challenges the library and community may face. For instance, issues that might indicate risk, such as the library's proximity to hazards (i.e., nuclear plant, construction, highway, etc.) or its location with regard to terrorist threats (adjacency to a large airport or city), will have an impact on how you prepare, whether you're located in Washington, DC; Washington, Kansas; Washington, Mississippi; or Washington, Maine. Other physical considerations, such as the potential for water damage (if you are in a flood zone, what is the age of your building's pipes?) and service provision (are there open stacks?) can also lead to informed planning and preparation.

Halsted, Clifton, and Wilson (2014) provide steps that can help guide the risk assessment process. These steps start with creating a team that can help identify possible hazards and perform a vulnerability analysis, such as the likelihood that a certain type of disaster might occur. Useful team members include the library director, the property or facilities and safety managers, the financial manager, the information technology manager, and at least one staff representative. Outside experts who may be called upon for assistance include the local emergency management office (which may be at the town, city, or county level), the fire department, the police department, the public works department, emergency medical services, utilities and telecommunications providers, neighboring organizations and libraries, FEMA, the American Red Cross, and the National Weather Service (as a primary resource for weather updates).

The next step is to examine the library's strengths and weaknesses. To do this, a simple "SWOT" matrix, such as the one in table 2.2, can work. With this approach, the library team identifies where the organization has assets and where improvements might be made. For example, in the top left square, strengths of an external origin might be something like close proximity to the local fire station. A threat of internal origin, in the bottom right square, might be the age of the fire suppression system. Performing this type of assessment as a team activity will lead to more input and a proactive approach to disaster planning.

TABLE 2.2
SWOT matrix

	Helpful	**Harmful**
External Origin	**Strengths** Example: proximity to fire station	**Weaknesses** Example: very old wooden building
Internal Origin	**Opportunities** Example: staff willing to be trained	**Threats** Example: age of fire suppression system

This SWOT exercise can help inform the next step, which involves identifying the library's assets and potential losses. When listing assets, remember to consider the unique talents that library workers may possess, though keeping in mind this may be time-specific, and the fact that individuals' responses to a disaster may be unpredictable. Conducting an insurance assessment and examining mitigation options are the final steps in the risk assessment process. The risk assessment should be regularly reviewed and updated.

There are a number of freely available resources for conducting risk assessments. FEMA's Ready site (www.ready.gov/risk-assessment) offers tools in the areas of business impact and natural, human-caused, and technological hazards. FEMA's HAZUS program (www.fema.gov/flood-maps/products-tools/hazus) is a nationally standardized risk-modeling methodology. Its free GIS-based software identifies high-risk areas for earthquakes, tsunamis, hurricanes, and floods, and can be used to map and quantify risk information like physical damage, economic loss, social impacts, and mitigation cost-effectiveness.

Another valuable resource comes from the Earthquake Country Alliance, which has created a downloadable matrix to make risk assessment easy at www.earthquakecountry.org/library/7_Steps_to_a_Disaster_Resilient_Workplace.pdf.

Though the risk of cybersecurity attacks, such as ransomware, may seem low in the library setting, such incidents have occurred. Public libraries in South Carolina, Indiana, and Tennessee have all been victims of cyberextortion. In South Carolina, the Spartanburg County Public Library (SCPL) refused to pay the $36,000 that was requested, since no sensitive data had been stolen, and there was no way to know if the data they got back would be clean. In Indiana and Tennessee, they did pay the fee demanded ($1,500 and $1,300, respectively). In both of these cases, their full backup files were old (three months and two years, respectively). Tips from these folks who have successfully dealt with such an attack include: have a regularly scheduled backup (some advocate every night, and off-site every thirty days) and be sure to fully test it; have strong password policies; provide training and reminders for staff about phishing e-mails, especially since these types of e-mails have become more and more sophisticated; and provide clear and open communication to your users.

The SCPL can serve as a communication model in a crisis like this one: they posted signs on the day of the attack and notified trustees, the city council, and media outlets, and they used social media to keep folks informed. They employed the library's emergency text notification to provide daily updates for workers for the ten days that followed. They also recommend buying lunch for the IT folks who have to work long hours to restore the library's systems (Landgraf 2018).

Before moving to the discussion of mitigation, the text box "Playing the Game" (below) introduces disaster-related games, which also provide a forum for introducing disaster preparedness.

Playing the Game

IT IS EASY to become overwhelmed or get bogged down in the enormity of disaster preparedness. You should consider using games as a way to start the process, and to alleviate some of the stress that can arise when dealing with the topic of disasters. Here are a few resources to get started, and they could also be used and shared as program opportunities for community education:

- American Red Cross (redcross.org/get-help/how-to-prepare-for-emergencies/emergency-preparedness-for-kids/disaster-preparedness-for-teachers.html)
  » Disaster preparedness resources for teachers and schools
    Pillowcase Project (grades 3-5)
    Prepare with Pedro (grades K-2)

- FEMA (ready.gov/kids/games)
  » Build a Disaster Kit game
  » Disaster Master game
  » Ready 2 Help card game, downloadable in English and Spanish versions
  » Prepare with Pedro, disaster preparedness activity book

- NLM (https://toxtown.nlm.nih.gov/science-classroom)
  » Resources for middle-school students on the environment and health
    Toxtown Science Classroom - lesson plans, interactive games, hands-on activities, videos, informational websites

- NOAA (www.ngdc.noaa.gov/hazard/kidsquiz/#/)
  » Kid's Hazards Quizzes on natural disaster preparedness

- Sesame Street (sesamestreet.org/toolkits/ready)
  » Let's Get Ready: Planning Together for Emergencies, toolkit for emergency preparedness
    multimedia resources for caregivers, educators, families, and communities

- UN Office for Disaster Risk Reduction (stopdisastersgame.org)
  » Stop Disasters! online game (primary audience is 9- to 16-year-olds)

In mid-February 2020, as COVID-19 was starting to make its way across the world, the *Washington Post* (Noack and Petrelli) reported a surge in interest in games focused on combating viruses; this spike in interest echoed a similar spike that took place during the 2014-16 Ebola outbreak in West Africa. Games of all types provide an outlet for dealing with stress and anxiety, so it is no surprise that their popularity would increase during a looming pandemic.

One of the best commercial board games that is geared toward medical challenges is *Pandemic*, which was named the best board game in 2009 by the Academy of Adventure Gaming Arts & Design and now has spin-offs like *Pandemic: The Cure* (Smith 2020). Other board games include *Healthy Heart Hospital*; *Infection: Humanity's Last Gasp*; and *Plague*. Games that are framed around disasters and disaster response have been around for some time; the 1980 game *Mt. Saint Helens Volcano* is an example of an earlier disaster board game that is still available and popular today.

Mitigation

In terms of disaster preparedness, mitigation is the process of reducing the risk of loss or harm. The Stafford Act of 2011 (introduced and discussed in chapter 1) allowed FEMA to set aside a small percentage of its annual spending for disaster mitigation, an action that has been described as the "first major attempt by the U.S. government to plan for disasters *before* they happened" (Bittle 2020, 5; italics in original). This was a prudent move, as research has shown that mitigation efforts can help save lives and create jobs; in addition, every dollar spent on mitigation efforts saves six dollars in recovery funds (Lightbody and Fuchs 2018). The savings are particularly realized from safety, protection of property, and continuity of services. Some examples of mitigation efforts include the raising of structures in flood-prone areas, reinforced tornado rooms, floodplain and hazard mapping, and the enforcement of building codes. Regular common sense and keeping up with routine maintenance (e.g., keeping drains clear) can often help keep damage from occurring with a minimal amount of effort.

Hazard mitigation is carried out on state, local, and tribal levels. FEMA offers pre-disaster mitigation grants for state, local, and tribal governments that are looking to implement disaster mitigation strategies before a disaster strikes. Nonprofit entities are eligible for a number of other grants as well, such as the Preservation Technology and Training Grants from the National Center for Preservation Technology and Training, the Sustaining Cultural Heritage Collections from the National Endowment for the Humanities, and National Historical Publications and Records Commission grants. The following text box, "Mitigation, Too?" provides an example of mitigation planning, operation, and funding after record flooding affected a public library.

Mitigation, Too?

IN JUNE 2006, a record-breaking flood occurred in upstate New York. At that time, it was the worst flood in the mid-Atlantic region since 1979; the Susquehanna River crested fourteen feet above flood stage. The National Guard was called in, and thousands were evacuated from their homes. There were sixteen fatalities and $1 billion in damage. The village of Sidney was particularly hard hit, and while its beloved public library fared better than many, the building was not spared. The library's basement filled with water, and the disaster recovery was a long process. Figure 2.2 shows the basement hallway during the flood event.

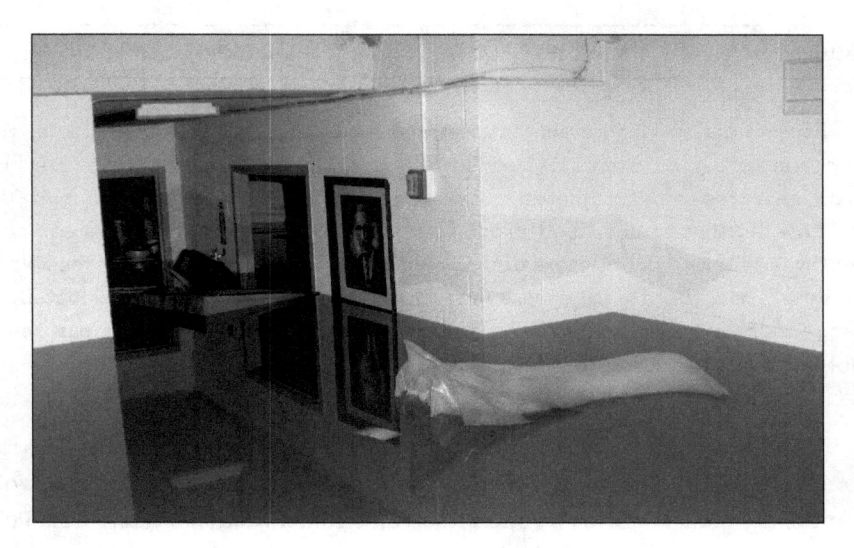

FIGURE 2.2
Flooding at Sidney Memorial Public Library

During the initial meetings with FEMA in summer 2006, it became apparent that the library was eligible for relief support in the form of financial reimbursement. The funds fell into the categories outlined in table 2.3 below.

For debris removal, and building contents and repairs, reimbursement occurred after the library had already expended the funds. In order to receive *any* reimbursement funds, however, the library also had to consider mitigation efforts and have a mitigation plan in place. At an initial assessment, FEMA advised that there were not any obvious adjustments that could be made to mitigate for future occurrences. A few months later, FEMA changed its recommendations and instigated the following mitigation measures for which it provided approximate funding: move the phone/computer lines, electrical boxes, and fire alarm system to the first floor; secure the oil tank; install backflow for downstairs plumbing; and "flood-proof" the boiler room.

TABLE 2.3
FEMA reimbursement

Fund Category	Reimbursement Amount	Date FEMA check received
Debris removal	$13,600	2/23/07
Building repairs	$54,586	4/26/07
Building contents	$49,419	6/14/07
Mitigation	$28,560	6/27/07

For mitigation reimbursement, estimates for these efforts were made, and funds were provided in advance to make the recommended improvements. The first three measures were completed in the second half of 2007. For the final two (the backflow installation and flood-proofing of the boiler room), the village engineer and three separate contractors determined that these efforts were not feasible at the time. Thus, there were excess funds that were received but not allocated, so these funds were returned to FEMA, hopefully to support mitigation measures at another library in the future.

This chapter has emphasized the importance of preparedness and disaster plans, and pointed to a number of resources for getting started. As we began with a cautionary quote, we will end on another, much older cautionary note from Publilius Syrus, a Latin writer of the first century BC, and his Maxim 469: "It is a bad plan that admits of no modification" (Bartlett 1992, 99). Once in place, every plan should be assessed and reviewed regularly and updated to reflect current environmental concerns, community needs, and local priorities.

REFERENCES

Associated Press. 2018. "What Goes into a Go-Bag? How to Prepare an Emergency Kit." *U.S. News & World Report*. www.usnews.com/news/healthiest-communities/articles/2018-06-12/what-goes-into-a-go-bag-how-to-prepare-an-emergency-kit.

Bartlett, John. 1992. *Familiar Quotations*. 16th edition. Boston: Little Brown.

Bittle, Jake. 2020. "On the Waterfronts." *The Baffler* 49, no. 1.

Halsted, Deborah D., Shari Clifton, and Daniel T. Wilson. 2014. *Library as Safe Haven: Disaster Planning, Response, and Recovery*. Chicago: ALA Neal Schuman.

Hunt, Kyla. 2020. "Hurricane/Tropical Storm Management." Texas State Library, "Library Developments." www.tsl.texas.gov/ld/librarydevelopments/2020/08/25/hurricane-tropical-storm-emergency-management/.

Landgraf, Greg. 2018. "When Ransomware Attacks: How Three Libraries Handled Cyberextortion." *American Libraries*, June 1. https://americanlibrariesmagazine.org/2018/06/01/when-ransomware-attacks/.

Lightbody, Laura, and Matthew Fuchs. 2018. "Every $1 Invested in Disaster Mitigation Saves $6." Pew Charitable Trusts. www.pewtrusts.org/en/research-and-analysis/articles/2018/01/11/every-$1-invested-in-disaster-mitigation-saves-$6.

McMahon, Jeff. 2019. "New Map Shows Expanse of U.S. Nuclear Waste Sites." *Forbes*, May 31. www.forbes.com/sites/jeffmcmahon/2019/05/31/new-map-shows-expanse-of-u-s-nuclear-waste-sites/#6b701b24c2cf.

Noack, Rick, and Stefano Petrelli. 2020. "Virus Games Are Going Viral as the Coronavirus Spreads." *Washington Post*, February 16. www.washingtonpost.com/world/2020/02/16/virus-games-are-going-viral-coronavirus-spreads/.

Smith, Monica M. 2020. "Disaster Board Games." Smithsonian Institution, Lemelson Center for the Study of Invention and Innovation. https://invention.si.edu/disaster-board-games.

Teper, Jennifer Hain. 2011. "Planning for Disaster Recovery in High-Density, High-Bay Library Storage." Presented at the International Symposium and Workshop on Cultural Property Risk Analysis, Lisbon, Portugal, September 14.

CHAPTER 3

The Human Element

Some hardships teach.
—*South African proverb*

DEPENDING ON A MULTIPLICITY OF FACTORS, SUCH AS SOCIOECONOMIC STATUS, geographic region, and so on, an individual or community might be more likely to experience one type of disaster over another; but disasters are in some senses equal opportunity events: they can strike anyone, anywhere, at any time. Disaster preparedness, response, and recovery efforts are at their core about people, their needs, their vulnerabilities, and their expectations. So, whether the task involves creating a disaster plan, identifying geographic risks, or overseeing rebuilding efforts after disaster strikes, attention to the human element is key in every step and consideration. At the library level this means, before disaster strikes, identifying community partners and vulnerable segments of the community, sorting out expected roles, and engaging in preparedness efforts. It may also mean lending support to community and staff on the individual level in the event of a disaster, and during the recovery process.

Ideally, preparedness and response efforts are about dedicated individuals working together toward a common goal: the community's well-being. The individuals who are involved in these efforts may come from a variety of institutional and organizational backgrounds, with differing goals and outlooks. Additionally, the library as an organization is a member of many communities, radiating out from the level of the local association (which might include schools, a university, consortium, village, town, city, state, etc.). Depending on the library's type and setting, state-level influences and even national and international factors may also play a role in the library's functioning and autonomy during a crisis.

Though each disaster, setting, and community may be unique, there are some commonalities in terms of how we as humans experience disasters that can help guide our response and recovery efforts. This chapter starts with a description of the collective psychological phases a community goes through during disaster response, and then covers individual responses to disasters, and ways to offer support. A discussion of disasters that are commonly caused by humans follows, including active shooters, bomb threats, arson, civil unrest, and the COVID-19 pandemic.

Phases of Disaster Response

The Disaster Technical Assistance Center (DTAC), part of the Substance Abuse and Mental Health Services branch of the U.S. Department of Health and Human Services, outlines six phases of disaster response that communities experience. These are framed by how the disaster commonly affects the attitudes, perspectives, and mental health of the people involved. The first phase, or the *pre-disaster* phase, is generally accompanied by uncertainty and the fear and anxiety which impending risk can evoke. Levels of warning differ with different types of disasters; for instance, an earthquake or a shooting may have little warning. Sudden events can engender feelings of inability to protect yourself and others, a general lack of security, and fear of the future. Disasters that afford some warning like blizzards and hurricanes may cause self-blame or guilt for not acting upon the warnings. The pre-disaster phase may take as little as minutes, such as a bomb threat, or may last many months, such as hurricane seasons.

The second phase, or the *impact* phase, is typically the shortest phase and consists of reactions during the actual disaster. During this period, people's psychological reactions can exhibit a broad range, though this is somewhat dependent on the type of disaster. This phase is typified by confusion and disbelief, followed by a focus on protection and self-preservation. In the immediate aftermath of a disaster event comes the third phase, described as the *heroic* phase. During this time there are often high levels of activity, a heightened sense of community, increased altruism, and high adrenaline levels (which may lead to impaired judgment). Like phase two, the third phase also occurs over a relatively short time period.

The DTAC calls the fourth phase the *honeymoon* phase, which commonly lasts a few weeks. This is an optimistic time, during which assistance is at hand and community bonding takes place. This phase allows for building relationships across the community. The stage that follows is markedly different: the *disillusionment* phase. During this fifth stage, which can last months, and sometimes years, the limits of disaster assistance become evident. This stage is characterized by increased stress, discouragement, and physical exhaustion. Trigger events, such as the first anniversary of the event, can exacerbate and extend this stage. The sixth or final phase is called the *reconstruction* phase, and can last for years. This stage is typified by adjusting to a new normal, and a feeling of recovery.

Individual Responses

While we have some knowledge of the phases a community generally moves through during disaster response and recovery, how individuals respond to disasters involves a combination of factors, some inherent and some not. Because disasters can have an impact on many levels, physically, socially, and psychologically, it is difficult, if not impossible, to anticipate how any one person will respond until the actual event takes place.

There will likely be different approaches and needs in terms of how the library organization can help affected individuals cope, whether they are staff members or the community served. The former requires plans to lessen the responsibilities and burdens on staff. The latter often involves providing different or extra services by the staff. Within the library team, the director or leadership can have a profound influence on the stress and well-being of the staff. There should be some formal consideration in advance for how to be supportive and attentive if disaster strikes. For example, arranging in advance the conditions under which hourly employees might be paid during a disaster when the library has to be closed can be profoundly helpful during an already stressful period. Other steps, such as having the supervisory staff adapt or change their work hours to make sure there is always a supervisor on duty while the facility is open (e.g., weekends), or dividing up the responsibility for regularly checking in with staff, may have to take place in a more ad hoc manner. Some of the library workers and regular volunteers may have specific characteristics (e.g., single parent, older individual who lives alone) that would logically place them higher on the management's check-in list. A plan for the most likely disasters in each setting should think through what the likely support needs of the staff are, while they work in the library both during or after the disaster, and what their needs are that will enable them to return to work when appropriate.

During the COVID-19 pandemic, we learned various coping mechanisms for the numerous challenges that arose. The University of North Carolina's School of Medicine (Cristy and Meltzer-Brody 2020) offered tips for dealing with staff stress, though these recommendations can be readily adapted to apply to all types of challenging situations. These tips include:

- Recognize that every individual reacts to challenges in their own way, and at their own pace.
- Regularly monitor individuals' reactions and performance for radical changes.
- Be flexible in scheduling and assignments.
- Modify and adapt your expectations to match individuals' abilities and personal challenges.
- Ensure that there are mechanisms created or in place to offer psychosocial support as needed.

The School of Medicine also offered Do's and Don'ts, as outlined in table 3.1 below.

TABLE 3.1
Do's and Don'ts

DO	DON'T
Discuss issues openly, and work to remove stigmas.	Show irritation when folks are struggling.
Explicitly ask how staff are doing.	Be inflexible or rigid.
Encourage awareness about the effects of stress.	Underestimate the effect of stressors on staff and yourself.
Manage and adapt expectations, since there are a wide range of coping reactions.	Make comparisons among the staff members.
Respect the fact that individuals move through phases at different paces.	Assume that everyone is "okay."

While library workers may not typically be classified as first responders, they may find themselves in the position of working with traumatized community members during or after a disaster event. Thus, the tips which have been outlined for first responders can also help guide staff members' interactions. These include promoting safety, calm, connectedness, self-efficacy, and help. Concrete ways to do this include:

- Provide clear, accurate information on the disaster, on relief efforts, and on where to obtain help.
- Be compassionate.
- Help people to contact their friends and family.
- Provide practical suggestions so that folks can help themselves.
- Offer up-to-date information on local and regional services.

Tips on things to avoid include giving simple, reductive reassurances (e.g. "don't worry, everything will be all right"); forcing people to share their experiences; making promises that might not be kept; and criticizing relief efforts in front of people who may be seeking out those same services (Department of Health and Human Services 2005).

Offering Support

Earl Johnson (2020, 187), who is one of the founders of the Spiritual Care function in the American Red Cross, and who helped create their Psychological First Aid curriculum, offers practical guidance and advice with ten "ways to comfort." Table 3.2, "Promoting Comfort," includes his suggestions in the first column; the second column adapts those suggestions for deployment in a library setting. Some of these suggestions are geared toward workers, and others are geared toward interacting with the library's community.

TABLE 3.2
Promoting Comfort

	Johnson's Ways to Comfort	Comfort in the Library
1	Thank a policeman or fireman today.	And/or thank your local EMT, library workers, etc.
2	Help a senior put together a go-bag.	Host a "how to build a go-bag" library program for varied demographic segments (virtual if needed).
3	Always have a flashlight handy.	Keep them at the front desk, in the elevator, etc.
4	Express gratitude to helpers in the community.	Create a library gratitude journal where staff can contribute their thoughts.
5	Clarify the situation and encourage hope.	Post positive progress regularly.
6	If it was wrong before the disaster, it is wrong during and after the disaster.	Systemic issues should be identified and addressed beforehand, as much as possible.
7	Children are not invisible and are impacted by disasters and need comfort.	Host programs and provide resources to support children and families.
8	Do not impose your cultural norms on others with different cultural norms.	Host programs and provide resources that serve *all* members of the community.
9	Talk to children honestly, but age-appropriately.	Host programs and provide resources that are age-appropriate; tailor them for the audience.
10	Ask about someone's family with care and no judgment.	Exercise compassion for *all* members of the community.

Note that the last half of Johnson's comfort suggestions in the table move toward the needs of the community. This may be due to the fact that crises have shown that the act of serving the community can bring enormous boosts in morale. A relatively straightforward way to invoke a spirit of community support and engagement during times of disaster is to promote opportunities for staff to engage in outreach and recovery efforts using their unique talents and assets, as described in the text box "After the Storm" by Christian Edwards, assistant keeper at the Wilson Special Collections Library.

After the Storm

BY CHRISTIAN EDWARDS, ASSISTANT KEEPER

North Carolina Collection Gallery, Wilson Special Collections Library,
University of North Carolina at Chapel Hill

WHEN HURRICANE FLORENCE hit North Carolina in mid-September 2018, it brought water and structural damage to the Indian Education Resource Center at the University of North Carolina at Pembroke. With power out for more than twelve days, the staff returned to find artworks molded and, they thought, lost forever.

As part of the state's volunteer Cultural Resource Emergency Support Team (CREST), I visited the center on October 12, 2018, to see what could be salvaged and returned to exhibit. The North Carolina Department of Natural and Cultural Resources organizes CREST to help institutions prepare for and recover from disasters.

Although our team had only four people, we each brought different talents to the job. So, we divided the work and set out to conquer a long list of tasks. When we arrived, many of the most damaged items were in a freezer to prevent additional deterioration and mold. These were some of the more challenging and fragile items to salvage. Our goals were to clean the objects, photograph the frozen textiles in preparation for conservation treatment, soak a stack of stuck-together photos to release them, and begin drying and cleaning various artifacts. Because the center was still so damaged, we moved the items to a nearby gym, working on large tables where we could spread everything out.

During the hurricane, the center's ceiling had collapsed. Plaster and building materials fell on everything, including a mounted buffalo head. The wet plaster dust had caked in the thick hair all around the head's sides and underneath. We vacuumed extensively and still could not remove all the particles.

A huge mural on canvas was fragile due to chipping paint and its overwhelming size. Painted for the 300th anniversary of Roanoke Island, this mural of Lumbee history held great meaning for the center. It took all four of us to flip the painting over so we could sweep dust from the back and lightly clean it with an alcohol solution.

THE HUMAN ELEMENT | 45

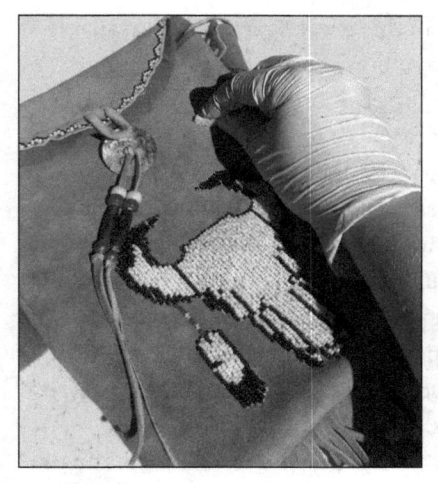

One team member organized scattered photos according to any clues she could find. The images came from multiple albums, and many were stuck together. I'm glad to say that out of the couple dozen that needed to be separated, only about five were unsalvageable.

The item that needed the most attention was a leather vest (shown in figure 3.1) that staff said was one of the most culturally valuable pieces at the center. Two weeks of sitting in a wet building had left the vest covered with green and black mold. Staff assumed that it was too far gone for salvage.

FIGURE 3.1
Cleaning artifacts

Because of its significance, CREST decided to attempt to save the vest. During a prior visit, volunteers had frozen it to halt the mold growth. As soon as our team arrived, we removed the vest from the freezer to thaw, and then we vacuumed it thoroughly. At the end of the day, the vest went to a textile conservator in Raleigh for evaluation and conservation.

In all, it was a long, arduous day that was nevertheless extremely satisfying for all of us. The center still has a long way to go to get things back up and running but when it does, it will have many of the original artifacts they feared the storm had taken from them forever.

This summary was originally printed in the UNC-Chapel Hill Libraries' publication WINDOWS *26, no. 3 (Spring/Summer 2019): 20–21.*

As we safeguard and salvage collections, we should also reflect on the history of how those collections were defined and how they evolved to reflect (or not) the *entire* library's community. While a detailed discussion of egregious historical misdeeds and collection issues is beyond the scope of this volume, in the event of rebuilding after a disaster, careful consideration on how to get input from the *entire* community the library serves should be sought, so that the rebuilding process and product reflect inclusive input and a community mindset. Though it was designed in response to the COVID-19 crisis, the resource "Library Staff as Public Servants: A Field Guide for Preparing to Support Communities in Crisis" (created by Mega Subramaniam and her colleagues at the University of Maryland's College of Information Studies) is a great tool to aid in this process. It is freely available at https://yxlab.ischool.umd.edu/projects/reimagining-youth-services-during-crises/.

Library workers may find themselves in the position of helping children cope with a disaster and its aftermath. A valuable resource for this is the volume by the education professor Cathy Grace and the early childhood policy analyst Elizabeth Shores: *After the Crisis: Using Storybooks to Help Children Cope* (2010). Though written in 2010, the book is still pertinent today. It includes guidelines for working with children who have experienced various traumas such as earthquakes, epidemics, mass casualty incidents, fires and explosions, hurricanes, floods, shelter experiences, tornadoes, and volcanic eruptions. The volume is filled with booklists, activities (e.g., art center options), discussion starters, and other materials for children ranging in age from 2 to 8 years.

The Centers for Disease Control and Prevention (CDC) now offers training for its employees in its Office of Public Health Preparedness and Response on using a trauma-informed approach to care during public health emergencies. The six principles of trauma-informed service are safety, trustworthiness and transparency, peer support, collaboration and mutuality, empowerment, and cultural, historical, and gender issues (CDC 2021). The CDC has a downloadable infographic with these six principles that could be posted as a ready reminder that using this type of approach is an ongoing process, and not just part of a checklist: www.cdc.gov/cpr/infographics/6_principles_trauma_info.htm.

Trauma-informed approaches to providing service are becoming more common in library settings as well. National and state library organizations, such as the Public Library Association and the North Carolina Library Association, have recently offered workshops hosted by licensed social workers on the topic. The workshops emphasize the importance of understanding the impact of trauma and how it affects individuals and their behavior, and provide ways for librarians to respond to the physical and psychological phenomenon of trauma and its effects.

The book *A Trauma-Informed Approach to Library Services* (2020) by Rebecca Tolley is a timely resource that outlines the six principles of trauma-informed service, and offers various tools for offering empathetic library service and positive patron interaction and support.

Man-Made Disasters

It is common to categorize disasters by their causation: natural or man-made. While this makes for easier study, discussion, and analysis, it is a simplistic way to make distinctions. Rather than falling into two distinct categories, disasters more likely fall along a continuum, as it is difficult to separate the natural world from the humans who inhabit it. For example, an argument can be made that the increasing frequency and strength of natural disasters are largely due to human activities, and humans' reactions and entrenched institutional structures and systems have a profound effect on how disasters are experienced. Having said that, there are disasters that can clearly be attributed to human causation, such as shootings, bomb threats, arson, and civil unrest. These generally occur within a shorter time frame and in a limited location; they often require short-term closure, emergency department (police or fire) assistance, and perhaps some type of additional support (e.g., counseling) for library workers.

Natural disasters and weather-related emergencies, on the other hand, typically affect a larger geographic area. Their physical effects are often longer lasting, but these types of disasters are also likely to afford more opportunities and access to widespread community support and services, be it federal, state, or local assistance. In natural disasters, providing support for the staff may entail locating counseling services, but it may also include things like identifying locations for tetanus vaccinations if library workers are involved in flood cleanup, and deciding on whether the library should serve as a vaccination center. Natural disasters are covered in chapter 5 of this book.

All types of disasters have lasting impacts and consequences that we might not anticipate or expect. Just as COVID-19 has starkly demonstrated social and health inequities worldwide, catastrophic events have regularly shown us that the ordinary ways our societies and cultures operate are far from optimal. Entrenched societal problems can be brought to the forefront with stunning clarity; one such example is the rise of family violence during and after disasters. After Hurricane Katrina in the United States, researchers found that the physical victimization of women increased from 4.3 percent to 8.2 percent in southern Mississippi, representing a 98 percent increase between the six months prior to the hurricane and the six months after the hurricane (Schumacher et al. 2010). After New Zealand's Canterbury earthquake in 2010, domestic violence increased by 53 percent; after devastating wildfires in Australia, women who lived in severely burned areas reported domestic violence rates at seven times that of women who lived in areas that weren't severely burned (Parkinson 2013).

Sometimes the adverse effects of disasters take longer to manifest themselves. In 2004, a 9.1 earthquake caused a widespread tsunami in Indonesia and the neighboring region, causing over 225,000 deaths. Fifteen years later, researchers found links between exposure to the tsunami and post-traumatic stress, along with increased indicators of poor cardiovascular health. Those who lived in areas with heavy damage had poorer health outcomes than those in areas with less damage (LaFaro 2021). The increase in domestic violence and women murdered by their intimate partners in Puerto Rico in the months following Hurricane Maria (2017) eventually led to the governor declaring a state of emergency over gender violence in January 2021 (Florido 2021).

These are just a few examples of the long-lasting effects and societal ripples that disaster events can cause. The library's complementary roles of providing information and information access while serving as a community support center can be leveraged to offer resources and services to community members who are struggling with the effects of catastrophic events.

Community Engagement

Just as disasters can starkly illuminate societal inequities and injustices, they can also demonstrate the importance of the library's connectedness to the community. It is crucial to try to anticipate ahead of time how the library can continue to serve its community during tumultuous periods. For example, if your library facility can be used for community members to meet with FEMA representatives after a disaster occurs, can you provide or adapt space for these meetings? If your facility can be used as a heating or cooling center during power outages, should you purchase and install generators? If your library is the primary internet access point in town, how can you sustain that access during a disaster? Should you, for instance, invest in a satellite-based access system? What might be the requirements and investments to keep the library open, and under what circumstances might the library close? Determining these things ahead of time will simplify response efforts immensely.

Volunteers

Depending on the circumstances of a particular disaster, it is likely that volunteers will step up to help out with recovery and response efforts. Having a plan for this can help leverage these assets. With clear duties that have been outlined ahead of time, volunteers can begin assisting immediately, with little time and momentum lost. In some libraries, the Friends group coordinated volunteer activities to help with cleanup efforts after flooding. You should keep track of volunteers' efforts and their hours logged during response activities; this will be helpful when it comes time to fill out FEMA forms during the recovery period. You should also remember to thank your volunteers, whether it is with a handwritten thank-you note, a commemorative T-shirt, a bookplate, or recognition on your website. After the experience of removing damaged carpet at a flood-ravaged library, one volunteer, wanting to get more involved, joined the library's board of trustees.

Other Duties, Assigned or Not

Before the COVID-19 pandemic hit, library workers were featured in the news because of their heroic efforts in response to the nationwide opioid epidemic in the United States. Across the country, library workers and security staff sometimes had to administer the recovery drug naloxone to individuals who had overdosed while at the library. There is ongoing debate about whether this task fits in a librarian's job description (Ford 2019), and rightfully so; but if someone is overdosing in the library restroom, there may not be time for debate.

The state of North Carolina has been particularly hard hit by the opioid epidemic and was labeled as "number one" due to its high rate of opioid-related deaths (More Powerful NC 2019). In 2020, a statewide survey of North Carolina public library directors found that *all* of the respondents reported that their communities had been affected by the opioid epidemic, and almost half reported that the opioid epidemic had a *direct* impact on their library's functions. Three-quarters of the respondents agreed that libraries should be involved in opioid epidemic response efforts, including the administration of naloxone. About 10 percent of the libraries had naloxone on hand, and 25 percent had given their staff training on naloxone administration. Some libraries reported close proximity to local emergency services (in one case, they shared a building) and could rely upon their support, without the need for library personnel involvement (Wrigley et al. 2020). In almost each case, the interviewed librarians had assessed the opioid crisis in their community, assessed their library's assets and value systems, and formed a logical, local response to this human crisis.

The opioid epidemic is yet another example of what some may refer to as "mission creep," or the expansion of duties due to the demonstration of previous successes. As libraries are increasingly relied upon to fill gaps in social support systems, each organization should engage its team in decision-making processes, offer ample and appropriate training when services have to be adapted, and honor individual workers' levels of willingness to expand their duties. If willing staff do step up, make sure that they have support mechanisms for these expanded tasks, and access to professional support (i.e., training and counseling) if necessary. No matter how the library responds or decides to respond in complicated situations such as these, county health departments and community health agencies can be indispensable partners for guidance on the library's response to public health challenges.

The next sections consider disasters that are more likely to be viewed through the lens of human causation, rather than inflicted by weather or nature: active shooters, bomb threats, arson, and civil unrest. The COVID-19 pandemic is also covered, even though it could be argued that it falls in the natural disasters category, due to the fact that it is an infectious disease.

Active Shooters

Regrettably, we can point to examples of libraries where an active shooter event occurred in their facility or in their community. An active shooter is an individual who is attempting to kill or is actively engaged in killing people in a confined and populated area. Active shooter situations are unpredictable, evolve quickly, and are usually over within 10–15 minutes. As with other types of emergency procedure drills, response steps should be outlined and explained in the disaster plan, and library workers should practice active shooter procedures regularly. There should be instructions for communication, evacuation, where to gather (including where to take patrons), and lockdown procedures. Consideration should be given to the facility's floor plan, with attention to assets (e.g., hiding places, escape routes) and vulnerabilities (e.g., open floor plans, doors with windows).

Because each facility will be unique, with different considerations, active shooter procedures should be explicitly tailored for each organization, and clear actions that should be taken should be provided. The main priority during an active shooter event is to prevent harm to potential victims, to the extent possible. Staff training can explain the three responses: run and scatter, hide if necessary, and fight if there is no other choice, and this training should be provided to all workers. If there are security personnel affiliated with your library or there are local law enforcement personnel who can provide training, invite them to lead a session for library workers. There are also videos available (with graphic sounds and images, so trigger warnings may be needed) to assist with the topic, such as "Surviving an Active Shooter" from the Los Angeles County Sheriff's Office. It is just over nine minutes long and is available on YouTube at www.youtube.com/watch?v=DFQ-oxhdFjE. Ohio State University's video with the same title is six minutes long, and is also available on YouTube, at www.youtube.com/watch?v=9Z9zkU--FLQ. Be sure to provide an opportunity to debrief after this type of training, with appropriate support mechanisms in place. Allow staff members to opt out of watching if needed, but make sure that they still understand the response procedures.

The Department of Homeland Security encourages a "whole community" approach to preparedness and offers resources geared toward first responders, human resources or security personnel, and private citizens. The department also provides access to an independent study course, an active shooter workshop at www.cisa.gov/active-shooter-preparedness. Professional conferences and continuing education workshops (e.g., the ALA annual conference, state library conferences) also offer opportunities for learning more about this difficult challenge. Such a session was reported on in *Library Journal*, where significant points were highlighted, such as turn off cell phones; do not pull the fire alarm, since this will cause people to run and become possible targets; and when police arrive, don't approach them, and keep your hands visible at all times (Sendaula 2016). Active shooter events can devastate a community, no matter the physical locale in which they occur. Librarians who have gone through this horrifying experience emphasize the importance of regular training to ensure that staff are well informed and patrons are protected.

Bomb Threats

At almost exactly the same time as the Boston Marathon bombings in 2013, fire broke out at the John F. Kennedy (JFK) Presidential Library and Museum. The origins of the fire were unclear, which led to media reports linking the fire with the bombings, and concern over possible further explosions. Early on, the police commissioner helped fuel the rumors, saying the JFK incident may have been linked to an incendiary device, even though the library director clearly stated that the fire was not from an incendiary device, and had started in a mechanical room.

The library's Twitter account sought to reinforce the point that the fire was not related to the Boston Marathon bombings: "Fire at @JFKLibrary today. All people are safe. Fire investigation underway. No info on damage yet. Any tie-in is speculation" (Forry 2013). This example is included to show that during an emergency event with a resultant climate of heightened anxiety, rumors can take on a life of their own. It is imperative to share clear, precise information, even though this may be overlooked initially. Ideally, planning can help identify mechanisms (e.g., the press officer in the mayor's office) that will have procedures to help deal with misinformation or contradictory reports. After an inquiry into the fire, it was determined that a construction worker had disposed of a cigarette improperly, causing the fire, and no small amount of concomitant panic.

While a bomb threat may seem unlikely, the library disaster plan should include steps to take in the event that one does occur. All bomb threats should be treated seriously until proven otherwise. Specific procedures for bomb threats are covered in chapter 5.

Arson

As with the example of the JFK Presidential Library cited above, unintentional fires often occur due to forces beyond our control, such as construction or renovation projects. Arson, or the deliberate act of setting a fire, is also beyond our control, and though it may not be possible to totally prevent fires no matter what their origin, there are preventive measures that can minimize exposure and damage. These measures include safeguarding collections ahead of time with digital copies of vital documents kept off-site; using fireproof document containers for irreplaceable items; installing fire doors and ensuring they are not propped open; conducting regular inspections to identify vulnerabilities; and keeping an updated map or floor plan so that it is easy to locate valuable items for immediate removal. Other advice includes a regular review of insurance policies to ensure adequate coverage; closing off in-building book returns from the rest of the building, or locating fireproof book drops outside; and installing and testing detection systems and fire suppression systems as warranted. You should cultivate a relationship with the local fire chief and the local fire department. Invite them for a tour of the library; they may help identify vulnerabilities, and in turn will become familiar with the facility.

Susan Orlean (2018) engagingly chronicles the largest library fire in U.S. history, the mysterious Los Angeles Public Library fire in 1986. The fire burned for over seven hours, reaching 2,000 degrees. A total of 400,000 books were destroyed, with damage to over 700,000 more; the library was closed for seven years. No one was hurt during the fire; its cause remains unknown. Fire as a hazard is covered further in chapter 4.

Civil Unrest

According to FEMA, civil unrest involves activities such as strikes, demonstrations, or riots that are disruptive and require intervention to keep the public safe. Civil unrest can occur in any type of community, with or around a variety of activities, such as peaceful protests, sports activities, concerts, and political events (Vernon 2008). In recent times, we have witnessed an escalation of civil disturbance or unrest across the globe.

The public libraries in Ferguson, Missouri, and Baltimore, Maryland, provide excellent examples of library workers' valorous efforts to serve their communities during periods of civil unrest. In the case of Ferguson, in 2014, the city was rocked by weeks of protests and sometimes violent riots after Michael Brown, an unarmed black man, was shot and killed by a white police officer. The National Guard was brought in when a state of emergency was declared. Through it all, the public library stayed open, using social media to advertise the library as a place to pick up water and check e-mail. After the local schools were forced to close, teachers used the library for their classrooms. The sign posted at the front desk summed it up: "During difficult times, the library is a quiet oasis where we can catch our breath, learn, and think about what to do next." The library had previously served as a crisis support center after tornadoes and as a heating center during extreme weather (Inklebarger 2014).

In Baltimore in 2015, huge riots and protests erupted after the death and funeral of Freddie Gray, a young black man who suffered mortal injuries resulting from rough treatment during police transport. Some neighborhoods resembled war zones, with cars and shops on fire, looting, and broken shop windows. Schools were closed, yet through it all, the public library branches stayed open. The facilities were unscathed and provided a safe space for lessons to take place, for the media to charge their batteries, and for the community to connect with one another (Cottrell 2015).

In May 2020, during protests in Minneapolis over the brutal police killing of George Floyd, an unarmed black man, the public libraries did not fare as well. Library buildings were vandalized and windows were smashed, including nine artisan-etched windows at the downtown Central Library. At the Hennepin County East Lake branch, locals covered over broken windows with a cardboard sign sporting hand-drawn hearts, stating, "Respect this community-owned library" (Olson 2020).

As we engage in disaster preparedness to ensure the protection of collections and physical facilities, we must also prepare for other types of crises, such as civil unrest. We can turn to the outstanding examples of the libraries in Ferguson and Baltimore to guide us; this means empowering staff by providing training on how to deal with unfavorable or adverse circumstances, and keeping libraries open to support communities (Chancellor 2017). It is likely that each of these examples involved relative successes built upon years of good will within the community.

It is fortunate that most libraries have been fostering such good will, and these examples remind us of the need to plan on how to use that rare asset during the unpredictable future moments when it will be needed the most.

Staff training may include de-escalation training, nonviolent crisis intervention, and basic first aid training. Commercial vendors and nonprofit organizations such as the American Red Cross offer courses. In larger organizations and university settings, there may be a department such as an Office of Emergency Preparedness that will provide this type of training. In smaller communities, the local emergency response team can be a resource.

COVID-19 Pandemic

The first pandemic in a hundred years has stretched every individual, organization, community, and government across the globe in unforeseeable ways. Libraries of every type in every setting had to quickly adapt to provide services in new and innovative ways. There are numerous accounts of library workers everywhere stepping up in creative and varied ways, from creating homework aids for parents in lockdown, to lifting restrictions on Wi-Fi and lending Wi-Fi hotspots, to virtual programming, remote book clubs, health services outreach, making personal protective equipment, regularly checking in with senior patrons via phone, and serving as vaccination centers. More examples and ideas from public library responses during the pandemic can be found in the book by editors Kathleen Hughes and Jamie Santoro: *Pivoting during the Pandemic: Ideas for Serving Your Community Anytime, Anywhere* (2021).

Considerations such as how long the virus can remain viable on different types of surfaces seemed critical, and in the early stages there were conflicting reports about this. Since those early days, we've learned much more about transmissibility; and even though surface transmission isn't as pervasive or significant as airborne transmission, it still needs to be considered, especially as new viruses challenge our established ways of processing and providing materials. What we have learned about the "shelf life" of SARS-CoV-2, or how long the COVID-19 virus can live on common library materials, is due to the REopening Archives, Libraries, and Museums (REALM) project (www.oclc.org/realm/home.html). REALM is a collaborative research effort between OCLC, the Institute of Museum and Library Services, and Battelle to analyze how materials can be treated to mitigate exposure to COVID-19. Since those early days, organizations have adapted their responses as they have seen fit, keeping in mind staff concerns and comfort levels.

Throughout the course of the pandemic, many groups and individuals have stepped up to codify challenges, responses, successes, and to provide support. The ALA's COVID-19 Recovery site (www.ala.org/tools/covid-19-recovery) offers a range of tools in the areas of advocacy and policy, education, data and research, and guidance for content and protocols. In the text box below, medical librarian Brenda Linares examines information access in the Latinx community during the pandemic, and offers specific resources as well.

COVID-19 and Information Access in the Latinx Community

BRENDA LINARES

THE COVID-19 PANDEMIC brought many issues related to information access to light. There was rampant distrust of government information, as well as concerns regarding specific populations and greater exposure to the virus, and lack of access to quality information. One issue in particular that came to light was the amount of misinformation and disinformation surrounding the virus, how an individual could be infected, and how the virus could be transmitted.

The main difference between misinformation and disinformation is that misinformation is shared regardless of any intent to mislead, while disinformation is shared deliberately. When it comes to misinformation and mistrust in the Latinx community, there are a lot of barriers that create increased exposure to misinformation and a mistrust of available information. For example, there are language barriers, when Latinx people cannot find credible and evidence-based health information in their language. It is also imperative to keep in mind that the Latinx community is not homogenous and that it is not just Spanish that may be spoken and understood; many in the Latinx community speak and understand indigenous dialects as their primary language. There is also a shortage of Spanish-speaking health care workers, and fact-checking organizations may not publish their work in Spanish or other indigenous dialects.

There is also mistrust of health care services and information, a mistrust rooted in historical injustices inflicted on Latinx people by health care professionals. Due to this fact, they are more likely to rely on family and friends for information. The information they receive might not be as accurate, but they may be more likely to believe it because it comes from someone they trust. The mistrust of government among Latinx in the United States and misinformation about the coronavirus have created a bigger barrier for educating and providing reliable, accessible health information. Additional fears that may lead to misinformation include the fear of getting tested, the fear of getting COVID-19 after being tested, and the fear of losing one's job. For many, the reluctance to get tested or seek treatment stems from fear of deportation in a community with a significant percentage of undocumented immigrants (Associated Press 2020).

In the case of COVID-19, a combination of both misinformation and disinformation compounded issues of health literacy for those seeking to better understand how to protect themselves from COVID-19. In the United States, Spanish-speaking immigrants are particularly affected by the negative health outcomes associated with low health literacy. The social determinants of health are the conditions in the environments in which people are born, live, learn, work, play, worship, and age, and these can affect a wide range of health, functioning, and quality-of-life outcomes and risks. Health literacy is one social determinant of health that has an exponentially greater effect on minority populations, including the Latinx community. Members of the Latinx community are often unaware of the resources available to them, and in many instances, the information may not be available in their language. Most health information is written at the tenth-grade level, while 50 percent of the Latinx community reads at or below a fifth-grade reading level (Doak et al. 1996).

In order to understand how to reach and provide useful health information to the Latinx community, it is important to reflect on where they get their information. People with low reading skills rely on television and radio up to five times more often than print information or the internet. Since the most accurate print information about COVID-19 is in English, this leads people to rely on word-of-mouth information such as social media postings. These postings can in many instances provide the wrong information.

When it comes to COVID-19 and the Latinx population, unfortunately, not a lot of evidence-based information is available in Spanish. For example, in a January 2021 search of the Johnson County, Kansas, public health department's website on COVID-19, we could not find any information about COVID-19 or the vaccine available in Spanish. This lack of access to information has dire consequences. Members of the Latinx community in the United States are now four times more likely than non-whites to be hospitalized because of COVID-19. There are other reasons for these disparities as well, including being less likely to have health insurance or access to quality health care, due to their immigration status, and being unable to afford health care services. The Latinx community also has a higher percentage of its population working in industries that are deemed essential and don't have the option of working remotely (e.g., food service, sanitation, meatpacking, construction, and retail). They also tend to live in larger, multigenerational households where social distancing is difficult.

In the face of all this misinformation and mistrust, here are some ways to reach out to the Latinx population. Aside from the vaccines, providing COVID-19 information that is understood by all Americans, regardless of their literacy level, is one of the best ways to make sure that we can stop the spread of the disease.

We need to be better prepared. Public health agencies need alternatives to standard print information for the tens of millions who have low literacy levels. We need to provide this information in diverse platforms such as social media and videos, and not rely just on the internet to disseminate information. Carefully written documents are important, but having them available only on the internet is useless for adults with low literacy levels because they may not be able to access them, read them, or understand the content. Ten percent of U.S. adults (nearly 33 million people) have no internet access and thus are not searching Google to find COVID-19 information. Therefore, we need to also consider the digital divide in the community, and information needs to be culturally sensitive. Librarians looking to undertake outreach efforts in this arena should consider finding community-wide partnerships and collaborating with community organizations to offer adult education programs. COVID-19 has taught us that it is important to have plans in place to help people get health information when they need it the most; that is, before an emergency strikes.

LIBRARIAN-RECOMMENDED COVID-19 SPANISH-LANGUAGE RESOURCES

JUNTOS Radio: Salud Sin Filtros (podcast with health topics, including COVID-19): https://juntosradio.podbean.com/.

NNLM Pacific Southwest Region COVID-19 Spanish-Language Resources: https://nnlm.gov/psr/guides/covid19_espanol.

MEDICAL LIBRARIAN-SELECTED COVID-19 SPANISH-LANGUAGE RESOURCES

https://docs.google.com/document/d/18TNTjiY-iUW4mxYCt5RZnkd2H15TZHPXARyEGN9_H-c/edit.

HealthReach (which includes the ability to search by language): https://healthreach.nlm.nih.gov/.

Rural Women's Health Project: https://rwhp.org/.

REFERENCES

Associated Press. 2020. "Latinos' Health Is Threatened by Coronavirus as well as Fear, Distrust." *NBC News,* August 14. www.nbcnews.com/news/latino/latinos-health-threatened-coronavirus-misinformation-well-fear-distrust-n1236732.

Doak, Cecilia C., Leonard G. Doak, and Jane H. Root. 1996. "The Literacy Problem." In *Teaching Patients with Low Literacy Skills,* 2nd edition. Philadelphia: Lippincott.

This chapter has examined the various human sides of disasters. In the final text box (below), "Seizing Opportunities," academic librarian Michele Hayslett describes her experience as co-chair of her university library's Emergency Preparedness Committee, and the importance of librarians' active involvement in emergency management.

Seizing Opportunities

MICHELE HAYSLETT
former co-chair, Emergency Preparedness Committee, UNC at Chapel Hill Libraries

LIBRARIES ARE NOT islands, and they seldom have emergency medical technicians or police on staff, so collaborating with community emergency response staff is crucial to prepare for eventual emergencies. In spring 2013, as co-chair of my library's Emergency Preparedness Committee, I heard from Campus Safety about an opportunity to host the annual campus-wide emergency response exercise in our library. This opportunity was exciting because the exercise is not just for our Campus Safety staff. The event always involves multiple community teams: community police, the county sheriff's department, community EMT teams, SWAT teams, hospital staff, and even safety staff from other area campuses. The event is usually held somewhere more isolated, in order to control access by nonparticipants and minimize the risk of someone mistaking the exercise for a real emergency. If held in the library, those teams would get to deal with issues specific to a highly trafficked location on the main campus.

I expected that getting approval from Library Administration would be tricky. Our library hardly ever closes. We needed to identify a time for the drill that would inconvenience as few library patrons as possible. We needed to identify ways to isolate the location of the drill in order to prevent accidental entry by nonparticipants, and to communicate about the drill to prevent misapprehensions about it being a real emergency. Finally and most importantly, we needed to sell our Library Administration on the benefits of the exercise for the library.

This last consideration turned out to be the easiest one to address: in a conversation with the associate university librarian, when she asked directly, "Why should we do this?" I responded, "Because it will help all of these different emergency responders get to know this building better." Since our library is the largest public building in the state, this was a compelling argument, and she agreed for us to volunteer our space.

The circulation staff, who keep daily gate statistics for those entering, told us that the one day of intersession between the first and second summer semesters had the lowest gate count every year, so that would be the best time to schedule the exercise. And in discussing scenarios with the campus exercise coordinator, we came to the conclusion that we could devote just the top two floors of the building to the drill: the top floor for the actual exercise, and the next floor down to use for staging equipment and responders. Since these floors primarily hold book stacks, they would have the least patron traffic. We could have library staff page any materials needed from those floors that day and otherwise restrict access to the exercise's participants.

Communication and collaboration were key. We worked with department heads to spread the word throughout the library about the exercise and limit library meetings and workshops scheduled in the building for that day. The Communications Office spread the word across campus through other communications staff and news notices, and created signage for that day to inform library users and casual passers-by both inside and just outside the building. Library Administration also approved staff volunteering to act as "victims" for the drill, which helped the EMT and hospital teams test their procedures. Other library volunteers were assigned posts in the elevator lobbies of the designated floors and in all stairwells just below those floors to prevent accidental intrusions; to sign in "victim" volunteers and process their signed "hold-harmless" releases (required by campus safety); and to greet building visitors throughout the day with information about the drill and to answer questions. Having walkie-talkies to communicate among the library volunteers (on a separate channel from the emergency teams) was an important component of our success on the day of the exercise.

Communication with the campus coordinator beforehand was also key. He would have much preferred to close the whole building for the drill so that the drill scenario could have included entering and exiting the building. Since Library Administration would not agree to this, participants were briefed that action on the first floor needed to be extremely limited, since nonparticipants would also be using that space. In another memorable conversation, the coordinator asked if they would be allowed to use a smoke machine for the exercise—on a stacks floor. Um, no.

The drill was a complete success. The participating teams got a real sense of the difficulties an actual emergency would present in this building, given having to climb the stairs to the eighth floor (no using elevators during an emergency!), and all the tiny study rooms and carrels they would have to search once they reached that floor. And having safety staff from other campuses involved meant that the lessons learned were directly shared with those campuses, a direct benefit to our wider academic community.

Lessons were learned on both sides. One detail of the original drill scenario called for a panicked staff member to pull the fire alarm upon discovery of a suspicious package. While this could not be implemented in the actual drill, we did talk through the implications that would follow. When asked what our staff would be doing an hour after the fire alarm went off, I replied, "Well, the fire alarm goes off pretty frequently, so the usual thing our staff do after evacuating the building is head out to get coffee or find another library building in which to work." I quickly found out that in a real situation involving criminal behavior, police would want to talk with all library staff to gather statements, and anyone leaving the scene would immediately incur special attention as a possible participant in the crime.

For me personally, the drill highlighted the difficult process for hospital staff of identifying unconscious or deceased victims, given how seldom people carry photo identification on their person. Rescued victims were usually separated from their belongings. Since hospital staff could not release patients' identities until positively confirmed, this would result in great difficulty in tracking victims, and hence in family members receiving timely and accurate information. I subsequently have made a lasting habit of always carrying my photo ID at work.

Attending to the human side of disaster preparedness and response can be challenging and time-consuming. Since they cannot be avoided or sidestepped, it's best to approach human interactions with an informed and thoughtful mindset, keeping in mind that each individual will perform and respond differently according to their unique gifts, challenges, and experiences. Opportunities for regular training and input, combined with an open communication pipeline, will help ensure that staff are prepared and empowered to respond positively if and when a disaster comes knocking or blows down the door.

REFERENCES

Centers for Disease Control and Prevention, Center for Preparedness and Response. 2021. "Infographic: 6 Guiding Principles to a Trauma-Informed Approach." www.cdc.gov/cpr/infographics/6_principles_trauma_info.htm.

Chancellor, Renate. 2017. "Libraries as Pivotal Community Spaces in Times of Crisis." *Urban Library Journal* 23, no. 1: article 2.

Cottrell, Megan. 2015. "Libraries Respond to Community Needs in Times of Crisis: Baltimore, Ferguson Just Two Recent Examples of Libraries Offering Refuge." *American Libraries*, May 15. https://americanlibrariesmagazine.org/2015/05/15/libraries-respond-to-community-needs-in-times-of-crisis/.

Department of Health and Human Services, Substance Abuse and Mental Health Services Agency. 2005. "Psychological First-Aid for First Responders: Tips for Emergency and Disaster Response Workers." NMH05-0210 Fact Sheet. https://store.samhsa.gov/product/Psychological-First-Aid-for-First-Responders/NMH05-0210.

Department of Health and Human Services, Substance Abuse and Mental Health Services Agency, Disaster Technical Assistance Center. 2020. "Phases of Disaster." www.samhsa.gov/dtac/recovering-disasters/phases-disaster.

Florido, Adrian. 2021. "Puerto Rico's Governor Declares State of Emergency over Gender Violence." *National Public Radio*, January 26. www.npr.org/2021/01/26/960855914/puerto-ricos-governor-declares-state-of-emergency-over-gender-violence.

Ford, Anne. 2019. "Other Duties as Assigned: Front-Line Librarians on the Constant Pressure to Do More." *American Libraries* 50, no. 1/2: 40–47.

Forry, Bill. 2013. "Police Probe Link between JFK Fire, Marathon Explosions." *Dorchester Reporter*. www.dotnews.com/2013/jfk-library-official-fire-not-related-marathon-attack.

Inklebarger, Timothy. 2014. "Ferguson's Safe Haven: Library Becomes Refuge during Unrest." *American Libraries*, November 10. https://americanlibrariesmagazine.org/2014/11/10/fergusons-safe-haven/.

Johnson, Earl. 2020. *Finding Comfort during Hard Times: A Guide to Healing after Disaster, Violence, and Other Community Trauma*. Lanham, MD: Rowman & Littlefield.

LaFaro, Alyssa. 2021. "Building Resilience for Storm-Battered N.C." *Endeavors*, February 2. https://thewell.unc.edu/2021/02/02/building-resilience-for-storm-battered-n-c/.

Miller, Annetta. 2005. "South African Proverb." In *African Wisdom for Life*. Nairobi, Kenya: Paulines Publications Africa.

More Powerful NC. 2019. "The Impact of Opioids." www.morepowerfulnc.org/get-the-facts/the-impact/.

Olson, Rochelle. 2020. "Hennepin County Tallies up Damage to Libraries, Service Centers in Last Week's Riots." *Star Tribune*. www.startribune.com/hennepin-county-tallies-up-damage-to-libraries-service-centers-in-last-week-s-riots/570968162/.

Orlean, Susan. 2018. *The Library Book*. New York: Simon and Schuster.

Page, Cristy, and Samantha Meltzer-Brody. 2020. "Principles of Disaster Psychiatry during COVID-19 Pandemic: What to Do Now." Presentation to staff, University of North Carolina at Chapel Hill.

Parkinson, Debra, and Claire Zara. 2013. "The Hidden Disaster: Domestic Violence in the Aftermath of Natural Disaster." *Australian Journal of Emergency Management* 28, no. 2: 28–35.

"REALM Test Results." 2021. *American Libraries* 52, no. 1/2: 32–33.

Schumacher, Julie A., Scott F. Coffey, Fran H. Norris, Melissa Tracy, Kahni Clements, and Sandro Galea. 2010. "Intimate Partner Violence and Hurricane Katrina: Predictors and Associated Mental Health Outcomes." *Violence and Victims* 25, no. 5: 588–603.

Sendaula, Stephanie. 2016. "Active Shooter Policies in Libraries: ALA Annual 2016." *Library Journal*. www.libraryjournal.com/?detailStory=active-shooter-policies-in-libraries-ala-annual.

Vernon, August. 2008. "Safe Response to Civil Unrest Incidents. *Fire Engineering*, March 1: 180–85.

Wrigley, Jordan, Caitlin Kennedy, Mary Grace Flaherty, Madison Ponder, Meg Foster, and Jesse Akman. 2020. "A Statewide Analysis of North Carolina Public Libraries and Their Response to the Opioid Epidemic." *Public Library Quarterly* 39, no. 5: 421–33.

CHAPTER 4

Our Natural Environment

If you do not heed the roar of thunder, you will be soaked by rain.
—*Sierra Leonean proverb*

"UNPRECEDENTED, RECORD-BREAKING, EXTRAORDINARY, SUPERLATIVE, UNPARALleled, historic, uniquely awful," and "relentless" are all terms that have been or can be ascribed to global weather these past few years. In 2020, in the United States alone, there were the most hurricanes and most named storms ever in one year. The last six years have been among the hottest ever, with the global average temperature about 2.2 degrees Fahrenheit warmer than the average from 1850 to 1900 (Fountain 2021). This warmer climate has contributed to widespread drought and more intense wildfires and has not been without immense costs, human and monetary. In the last five years, the United States has spent $500 billion on climate-related disasters, and $750 billion in the last two decades (Gaul 2019).

Generally speaking, different regions have varied challenges when it comes to the likelihood of disasters. In the United States, while earthquake risk is very high along the California coast and in southern Alaska, there also are risks in some eastern states and parts of the Midwest as well. Hurricanes are most common on the East and Gulf Coasts. Tornado risk is highest in the Midwest, but tornadoes have occurred in every state. Wildfire risk tends to be higher in the western parts of the country, but again, wildfires can occur almost anywhere with the right conditions. The likelihood of particular types of events in your region should be examined on a spectrum from what is highly likely to occur to what might be rare, so that resources toward planning and response can be allocated accordingly. This process can be part of conducting a risk assessment, as described in chapter 2.

This chapter will discuss the most common weather-related disaster challenges such as hurricanes, tornadoes, fires, and floods, and because so much about the planning for earthquakes is similar, they will be discussed here as well. For each type of challenge, we have included summaries of interviews with librarians who have guided their communities through a disaster event; referred to as "field reports," these summaries were crafted by Katherine Greene. The field reports are followed by pointers to resources for each specific type of event. These resources are meant to complement those for disaster planning that were given in chapter 2 (i.e., fema.gov, redcross.org). The sections in this chapter provide extensive resources and tools for addressing specific types of weather-related disasters.

Hurricanes

Hurricanes are storms with violent winds (minimum of 74 mph), usually accompanied by torrential rain, lightning, and thunder. More than 127 million people live in coastal communities in the United States; this means that about 40 percent of the U.S. population faces the threats that hurricanes bring (LaFaro 2021). This also means there is at least $3 trillion worth of property that is now at risk of flooding and catastrophic storms (Gaul 2019).

Hurricanes are categorized according to their strength and potential for damage using the Saffir-Simpson Hurricane Wind Scale (National Oceanic and Atmospheric Administration 2021), as shown in table 4.1. Hurricanes in category 3 and above are considered major hurricanes. Keep in mind that the Saffir-Simpson scale does not take into account some of the other hazards which often accompany hurricanes, such as storm surges, tornadoes, and flooding.

TABLE 4.1
Saffir-Simpson Hurricane Wind Scale

Category	Sustained winds	Types of damage
1	74–95 mph; 119–153 km/h	Very dangerous winds: some damage
2	96–110 mph; 154–177 km/h	Extremely dangerous winds: extensive damage
3	111–129 mph; 178–208 km/h	Devastating damage
4	130–156 mph; 209–251 km/h	Catastrophic damage
5	157 mph +; 252 km/h +	Catastrophic damage

Besides more frequent and stronger hurricanes in recent decades, the nature of hurricanes has shifted. Now conditions have become more favorable for superabundant rainstorms, and strong storms linger for days. In addition, increased development has led to less hydrologic capacity to accommodate the deluges that storm waters bring. That is, development tends to remove forests and increase developed land surface. These developments produce more storm run-off in the hours after the storm, and make stormwater management more difficult.

Through the subsidization of extensive development, federal and state programs have made the U.S. coastlines what they are today: an exceptionally high-value and vulnerable element of our collective natural disaster exposure nationally. This subsidization has been in the form of inexpensive financing, tax breaks, and heavily subsidized flood insurance, and has resulted in shifting the risk of building from the private to the public sector. In 1955, taxpayers covered 5 percent of the cost of rebuilding after hurricanes; now that number is approximately 70 percent, and it can sometimes be up to 100 percent (Gaul 2019). Thus, in the United States we have created and are repeating the same cycle of intense hurricanes, federal payouts, and more damage. To break this cycle, we need a more resilient approach.

Paul Ferraro, a professor at Johns Hopkins University, offers steps we can take on a societal level in order to prepare for the next overwhelming hurricane:

- Stop building and rebuilding in places with repeated flooding.
- Start and keep investing in green infrastructure to help manage storm-water runoff.
- Face the science and implications of climate change, which means that extreme weather events will occur more frequently.

How do these actions relate to the folks who use and work in libraries? Through information and programs, library workers can help communities consider how they might collectively help address the causes and effects of climate change, which has an effect on all types of weather-related disasters. Here are a few ways that libraries might help to influence the adoption of these steps:

- Provide programs and offer library meeting rooms for forums where these issues can be presented and discussed.
- In the process of building and rebuilding, consider the impact of this approach on long-term environmental well-being.
- Become involved in community planning efforts, and learn about zoning issues that affect the community's well-being. This involvement can be as modest as having relevant links available on the library website, or having maps displayed showing which areas were flooded in recent events.

What follows next is our first field report in this chapter. It is based on the account by library director Steven Williams of the effects of Hurricane Harvey on the Port Arthur Public Library in 2017.

Field Report from Port Arthur, Texas: Hurricane Harvey

THE CITY OF Port Arthur, which lies just on the Texas side of the Texas-Louisiana border in Jefferson County, did not expect to be severely impacted by Hurricane Harvey in 2017. The storm first made U.S. landfall in the early morning of Saturday, August 26, when it reached San Jose Island as a Category 4 hurricane, just northeast of Corpus Christi. As it moved further inland, Harvey weakened into a tropical storm but stalled for two days, dropping buckets of rain and causing flash flooding throughout Houston. While Port Arthur was certainly wet, meteorologists focused on the high wind speeds and flash flooding in the metropolitan area, thinking Houston would bear the brunt of the storm; nobody expected Texas to be hit twice. Harvey, however, had other ideas. After retreating back into the Gulf of Mexico and regaining strength, Harvey made landfall near Cameron, Louisiana, about 40 miles from Port Arthur on Wednesday, August 30. Towns in Jefferson County received 60 inches of rain, most of which fell on August 29 and 30, making Harvey one of the worst tropical cyclones in U.S. history.

The residents of Port Arthur did not know that they should prepare for such a record-breaking storm, and this made its effects even worse. The staff at the Port Arthur Public Library had no idea that when they returned to work on Friday, September 1, they would find a building flooded with up to two feet of dirty sewer water which had destroyed much of the library's contents. Books, movies, magazines, and audiobooks shelved less than two feet above the floor were destroyed, along with chairs, couches, desks, tables, and the shelving units themselves. All of the library's technological equipment—desktop and laptop computers, monitors, printers, projectors, microfilm machines, scanners, and cameras—was also destroyed. The building's HVAC system was damaged, and the library's local history collection of photographs, documents, and microfilm had also been affected (figure 4.1).

FIGURE 4.1
Inside the Port Arthur Public Library

Shortly after the storm, the library's parking lot was filled with tents to provide temporary shelter for homeless and displaced people when there was nowhere else for them to go. Like much of the rest of Port Arthur and greater southeastern Texas, the library had been put into a wringer that would take years to emerge from. Recovery efforts at the library could not begin right away. In the first few days after the storm, the community's focus was on rescuing those still stuck in flooded homes. The library staff, in addition to assessing the needs of their own families, worked with first responders and other critical city officials to do whatever they could to help the community.

Once it was the library's turn to receive assistance (figure 4.2), the first step was to remove the collection—approximately 145,000 items—to a climate-controlled space; everything wet was literally thrown into box after box and taken first to the armory down the street, and then to the Port Arthur Civic Center for evaluation. About 55,000 items had been destroyed, and librarians also used this opportunity to weed 30,000 additional items from the collection. Historical materials were sent away to be digitized. What items remained were then sterilized, dehumidified, vacuumed, organized into new boxes, palletized, shrink-wrapped, and sent to a climate-controlled, longer-term storage unit while the library was rebuilt.

Behind the library, trailer offices had been set up to provide work spaces for staff while they photographed the damage and researched costs for an eventual insurance claim. When the library building had been constructed in 1980 it was a modern, 25,000-square-foot space, but by 2017 it was beginning to show its age. After the destruction wrought by the hurricane, only the library's core framework was allowed to remain, and staff were faced with the monumental and bittersweet task of rebuilding the facility almost from the ground up. Fortunately, the library was well insured and had a director, Steven Williams, who was willing to fight for every dollar

FIGURE 4.2
Outside the Port Arthur Public Library

of reimbursement. This money was used to rebuild the library and replace collection items, equipment, and furniture. The library also applied to FEMA for funding to fix the parking lot once the "tent city" was no longer needed, but much of the recovery budget came from the insurance payout.

Phone and internet service was lost for many of the areas affected by Harvey, and the library in Port Arthur was certainly no exception. However, since the disaster was so widespread that the entire region was affected, notifying the public of the library's situation was not immediately necessary, since the library was not the primary focus for the community. Once service was restored, the library documented its recovery process, collection needs, and timeline for reopening via its website and Facebook page, as well as the city website, local newspapers, and any other conceivable resource. While the library was closed to the public, patrons were still able to borrow electronic materials, as well as items from neighborhood libraries, via the TexShare card program, which connects hundreds of libraries across Texas. Port Arthur librarians also worked to address misinformation that spread online and connect people to whatever government or local services they needed.

As the rebuilding process got underway, proposals for salvage and construction projects were bid on by local companies. New rooms were added to give the library building additional much-needed gathering spaces, the roof was replaced, and lighting was added to the parking lot outside. A fire suppression system was installed, and the HVAC and plumbing systems were repaired. More shelving was added to allow for collection growth, more computers were made available for patron use, and more electrical outlets were installed. An interior designer was hired to brighten up the space with color and make it more comfortable with seating and work areas. Overall, the library took advantage of a rare opportunity in which it was given the time and budget to consider every aspect of its space and make it as welcoming and efficient as possible. Grant funding and support from local Boy Scouts enabled the exterior landscaping to receive a makeover as well. In March 2019, after a closure of nineteen months, the Port Arthur Public Library was finally able to reopen.

Before Hurricane Harvey, the Port Arthur library did not have a disaster plan, but Director Steven Williams is now working to create one with the knowledge gained and mistakes made between 2017 and 2019. In reflecting on the storm and its aftermath, he highlighted two important things to consider when faced with such an ordeal: having a comprehensive inventory, and taking the recovery process slowly. The moment when everything on the floor has been damaged or destroyed by floodwater and is being taken out of the building is not the time to create an inventory. It is much more manageable and efficient to document shelving units, furniture, technology, and even decorative items as they are acquired, and it is especially important to document their cost for future insurance claims. Williams also advises that recovery projects be taken slowly; while it is certainly desirable to be able to reopen the library for normal service as soon as possible, rebuilding should not be undertaken lightly. With a disaster of the magnitude of Hurricane Harvey, organizations and residents across much of the Gulf Coast area were also working to rebuild and did not return to normal for a considerable time afterward. The pace of recovery does not need to be at a fever pitch; there is time to do it right. There is only one opportunity to rebuild after a disaster, and it must be done well so that the library can best serve its community in the future.

Resources for Hurricane Planning

A great starting place for information on hurricane preparedness is the National Oceanic and Atmospheric Administration, or NOAA (www.noaa.gov/), which houses the National Hurricane Center (www.nhc.noaa.gov/) and the National Weather Service (www.weather.gov/). These agencies offer a variety of checklists, tools, kits, maps, and information on current threats.

The principal strategy for addressing the risks of storm surge and flooding to your library facility is its physical location or placement, and this cannot be easily changed. The average library building is estimated to be approximately seventy years old, and oceans have risen and storms have intensified since that building's placement. Resources like the NOAA link above have current maps to enable your library to assess the risks as they currently exist, which may be far greater than the building's history might suggest. NOAA's portal (www.noaa.gov/education/resource-collections) includes links to a plethora of educational tools such as a high-school environmental science curriculum on hurricane resilience, lessons on hurricane mapping and charting winds (for middle school and high school students), various webinars, and so on.

The Florida Division of Emergency Management is another helpful resource for hurricane preparedness tools (www.floridadisaster.org/hazards/hurricanes/), with various links to help with supplying and preparing your home, checklists, and business and evacuation plans. The site also provides information on determining whether you are in a storm-surge zone by county for Florida residents. Check your own state's equivalent agency for similar state-specific resources.

For an engaging treatise and more information on the topic of the U.S. coastline, see *Geography of Risk: Epic Storms, Rising Seas, and the Cost of America's Coasts* by Gilbert M. Gaul (2019).

Tornadoes

Tornadoes are vertical funnels of air that are spinning very rapidly. They are often spawned during severe thunderstorms, and are sometimes accompanied by hail. They can last from minutes to hours, and sometimes they sound like the roar of an approaching train. The winds from tornadoes can exceed 300 miles per hour, and tornadoes have been known to leave a path of destruction up to a mile wide and 50 miles long. In the United States there are about a thousand tornadoes every year, and they occur more commonly in the spring. Though tornadoes most often occur in the Great Plains and the southeastern part of the country, as mentioned earlier, they have been reported in every state. While weather reporting has become much more reliable over time, tornadoes are still hard to predict, and they can occur at any time of day and at any time of the year.

The National Weather Service outlines a series of preparedness actions for tornadoes. The first is to be "weather-ready" by monitoring local alerts and by signing up for notifications. Some communities use sirens to warn of the likelihood of a tornado, while others issue alerts through local and regional media and by smartphone. The other preparatory steps are to create a communications plan, and to practice the plan. The plan should identify a safe place within the facility if possible (e.g., a basement, storm cellar, or interior room on the lowest floor with no windows) or a nearby safe building. Have regular drills so that everyone is familiar with the routine for moving to the appropriate part of the building. You should consider reinforcing a room if there is no safe room. FEMA provides plans for how to install a safe room at www.fema.gov/emergency-managers/risk-management/safe-rooms/resources.

A particularly dramatic example of disaster and recovery is described in the next field report from Tennessee, where the Lawrenceburg Public Library was devastated by a series of tornadoes.

Field Report from Tennessee:
Tornadoes at the Lawrence County Public Library

THE AFTERNOON OF Wednesday, February 5, 2020, was stormy in Lawrenceburg, Tennessee. A line of strong thunderstorms was moving through the middle of the state toward the northeast, but residents along its path were unaware that they would soon be in for much worse. The closest weather surveillance radars were in Nashville and Huntsville, Alabama, but neither adequately covered Lawrenceburg, leaving it vulnerable to sudden severe developments. With no warning, a tornado touched down at 5:56 p.m. in neighboring Loretto and caused havoc for ten minutes before dissipating. Moments later, another tornado began and made a beeline for downtown Lawrenceburg. The Category 1 storm traveled almost 11 miles in 11 minutes, destroying trees, power lines, and roofs along the way, and passed directly over the Lawrence County Public Library. According to the Enhanced Fujita scale that rates tornado intensity, wind speeds in a Category 1 tornado—generally considered "moderate"—can range from 86 to 110 miles per hour; the Lawrenceburg storm's peak wind speed was 100 miles per hour. By eight o'clock Wednesday evening, four additional tornados would develop as the weather front continued northeast and out of Tennessee.

Back in Lawrenceburg, the library was scheduled to remain open until eight o'clock. As the tornado approached, there were only two patrons in the building, and the two librarians on duty ushered them into a hallway with no windows. By the time they were able to situate themselves, however, the storm had already passed; thankfully, the patrons and staff were uninjured. Unfortunately, the building was not so lucky, and the roof sustained serious wind damage. Rainwater poured inside and ceiling tiles and insulation littered the floor (figure 4.3). There was no electricity, and since it was after sunset, it was too dark to be able to see much. Landline phones were rendered useless because of the power outage, but the staff used personal cell phones to notify the library director and summon county officials. Later that evening, the director, assistant director, county executive, and county maintenance crew evaluated the damage to the roof and moved some of the more valuable local history books to a safer area of the building. Beyond this effort, there was little that could be done in the dark.

The next morning, an insurance representative arrived to evaluate the damage and prepare a claim. In daylight, Director Teresa Newton could see that roofing shingles and tar paper had been blown away, and that ceiling tiles continued to fall. More than 1,500 books had to be thrown away, and computers, printers, barcode scanners, and receipt printers had been destroyed. A microfilm reader was damaged, as well as tables, chairs, some bookshelves, and other pieces of furniture. Restoration experts at ServPro were hired by the insurance company and

FIGURE 4.3
After the tornado, Lawrence County Public Library

by noon, workers had already set up dumpsters around the library, begun drying out the inside of the building, and boxing up what materials they thought could be saved. Most of the insulation and the ceiling tiles throughout the building were removed (and were eventually replaced) before they could fall and disintegrate. While ServPro employees were working, nobody else—not even library staff or county officials—was permitted to be on-site. Each day, however, the library director walked around the property with other stakeholders to supervise the progress.

Electricity returned to downtown Lawrenceburg two days after the tornado; until then, all business was conducted through cell phones. The return of internet connectivity meant that the library could inform the community about what had happened through its website and Facebook page. Local newspapers and radio stations also shared updates on the library's progress. City and county residents were a major source of support while the library was closed: a branch library in Loretto maintained service and temporarily adopted Lawrenceburg patrons, neighbors donated time and money to help rebuild, and there was great appreciation for the library and its services overall. The Loretto library also handled the return of books that had been checked out from the Lawrenceburg library before the tornado, and stored them until renovations were complete. Lawrence County was responsible for much of the logistical work required to fix the library: county officials interacted with insurance representatives, ServPro employees, roofers, cleaners, and so on. A temporary building was rented by the county for use while the library was under construction; this new space was used to prepare for future programs and displays, process new materials, and store what materials had been returned to the Loretto library but belonged in Lawrenceburg. Support from the county also allowed the library to take advantage of a work-release program at the local jail, in which inmates were brought to the library to contribute unskilled labor. Groups of inmates moved furniture into storage, moved shelving units out of the way, removed soiled carpeting, transitioned the space to LED lighting, and cleaned the entire library. Director Teresa Newton reflected that this was a very positive experience on both sides: the library benefited from another source of labor and librarians enjoyed getting to know the inmates, and the inmates took great pride in their work for the community.

An unexpected obstacle that delayed the library's recovery was the coronavirus pandemic, which began to significantly impact the United States in March, just one month after the tornado. Manufacturing delays affected the installation of new flooring in most of the library, and Lawrenceburg patrons had just grown accustomed to using the Loretto library when the county's departments—including libraries—were closed due to the pandemic. When it became possible, Loretto librarians shifted to curbside pickup options and continued to serve Lawrenceburg patrons. Once work was finally completed at the Lawrenceburg library, the final task was to put the books back on their shelves. There were several hundred boxes to empty, and while each box contained books that came from the same area, it took about six weeks of organizing and reorganizing to make sure that everything was in the correct order and fit on the correct shelves. Additionally, there were still some books with water damage that ServPro had overlooked and which could not return to circulation, and other materials which had been saved were weeded and disposed of as well. On June 16, more than four months after the February 5 tornado, the Lawrence County Public Library reopened to the public; because of the pandemic, service was limited to curbside pickup, but the community was excited nonetheless.

Although the library had a disaster plan at the time of the tornado, Director Teresa Newton noted that it was very outdated and she plans to update it. There was not a phone tree to distribute the effort of notifying staff immediately after the disaster, but the capability for group texting was a mitigating factor. There was also no prepared contact information for restoration companies or contractors, but this, too, was not needed, since the county took responsibility. It should be acknowledged, however, that while the county's involvement was very helpful and appreciated by the library, it came with additional challenges—namely, communication. Newton met with insurance agents and other officials during her daily walk-throughs and corresponded with ServPro employees, contractors, and county representatives, but she was often out of the loop when progress was being reported and payments were due. In the end, all the stakeholders were satisfied and everything was paid for (and, if possible, reimbursed), but at times the lack of communication was frustrating for library staff. Perhaps the most important thing Newton will incorporate and maintain in her disaster plan is an inventory, particularly of the library's technology. When replacement computers were brought in and set up, staff recorded the brand, model, and age of the computers, as well as all the software installed. The information on barcode scanners and printers is also now included. Furthermore, Newton intends to have a photographic inventory and video tour of the library that can be safely stored off-site; she underscores the fact that these resources would have been very helpful after the tornado, both to be able to see what might be missing or damaged and to see how furniture had been arranged before the storm. Even so, the library has fully recovered and now appreciates the support of a grateful community. Lawrenceburg has since installed a local weather radar.

Resources for Tornado Planning

The U.S. National Weather Service (www.weather.gov/safety/tornado) offers a range of information on its tornado safety site, from current tornado watches and how to prepare, to what the difference is between a tornado watch and a warning, to survivor stories and lightning safety. This site offers a comprehensive starting point for tornado preparedness.

The National Child Traumatic Stress Network (www.nctsn.org/what-is-child-trauma/trauma-types/disasters/tornado-resources) is funded by the U.S. Department of Health and Human Services, and is coordinated by Duke University and the University of California at Los Angeles. The network offers information and resources on a wide variety of disasters, including tornadoes. It provides handouts, fact sheets, tip sheets, and activities to help individuals and families prepare for and cope with tornado events.

Earthquakes

When two blocks of the earth's crust suddenly slip past each other along a fault line, the result is an earthquake. Some earthquakes have foreshocks, or smaller quakes that happen before the main earthquake, or mainshock, occurs. Mainshocks are always followed by aftershocks. Depending on the size of the mainshock, aftershocks can occur for days, weeks, or even years after the initial earthquake (U.S. Geological Survey 2021).

Two commonly used scales to measure earthquakes are the Modified Mercalli Scale (MMS) and the Richter Scale. The U.S. Geological Survey relies on the linear MMS, which is used to describe the *intensity* of the ground-shaking caused by the earthquake, as shown in figure 4.4.

Intensity	Shaking	Description/Damage
I	Not felt	Not felt except by a very few under especially favorable conditions.
II	Weak	Felt only by a few persons at rest, especially on upper floors of buildings.
III	Weak	Felt quite noticeably by persons indoors, especially on upper floors of buildings. Many people do not recognize it as an earthquake. Standing motor cars may rock slightly. Vibrations similar to the passing of a truck. Duration estimated.
IV	Light	Felt indoors by many, outdoors by few during the day. At night, some awakened. Dishes, windows, doors disturbed; walls make cracking sound. Sensation like heavy truck striking building. Standing motor cars rocked noticeably.
V	Moderate	Felt by nearly everyone; many awakened. Some dishes, windows broken. Unstable objects overturned. Pendulum clocks may stop.
VI	Strong	Felt by all, many frightened. Some heavy furniture moved; a few instances of fallen plaster. Damage slight.
VII	Very strong	Damage negligible in buildings of good design and construction; slight to moderate in well-built ordinary structures; considerable damage in poorly built or badly designed structures; some chimneys broken.
VIII	Severe	Damage slight in specially designed structures; considerable damage in ordinary substantial buildings with partial collapse. Damage great in poorly built structures. Fall of chimneys, factory stacks, columns, monuments, walls. Heavy furniture overturned.
IX	Violent	Damage considerable in specially designed structures; well-designed frame structures thrown out of plumb. Damage great in substantial buildings, with partial collapse. Buildings shifted off foundations.
X	Extreme	Some well-built wooden structures destroyed; most masonry and frame structures destroyed with foundations. Rails bent.

FIGURE 4.4
Modified Mercalli Intensity Scale

By contrast, the Richter Scale is a logarithmic scale that measures the energy released or the seismic waves generated by the earthquake. This scale describes the size, strength, or *magnitude* of the earthquake. Table 4.2 shows Richter magnitude and consequent effects.

TABLE 4.2
Richter Scale and effects

Richter Magnitude	Earthquake Effects
0-2	Not felt by people
2-3	Felt a bit by people
3-4	Ceiling lights swing
4-5	Walls crack
5-6	Furniture moves
6-7	Some buildings collapse
7-8	Many buildings destroyed
8+	Total devastation of bridges, roads, buildings

In terms of immediate response guidelines, the phrase "Drop, cover, hold on" is a familiar reminder where earthquakes are common. There are some ways to help safeguard facilities and homes, such as anchoring items into wall studs and moving heavy objects to low shelves. The CDC offers a handy infographic that outlines a number of helpful preparedness steps whether you're at home, in a car, or outside (www.cdc.gov/cpr/documents/BeReady_Earthquakes.pdf). It also has similar one-page graphics for other emergencies available for public use.

In Alaska, some communities use a portable earthquake mobile to simulate the effects of earthquakes at different magnitude and intensity levels. Other earthquake preparedness activities might involve book and discussion groups, especially if there are longtime community members who can share lived experiences, such as the 1964 Alaska earthquake described in the next field report from the Chugiak-Eagle River Library in Anchorage, Alaska, where they experienced a 7.2 magnitude earthquake in 2018.

Field Report from Anchorage, Alaska:
Earthquake at the Chugiak-Eagle River Library

ON THE SHORTEST day of the year (the December solstice, typically on or about the 21st of the month), the city of Anchorage, Alaska, only receives about five hours of sunlight. The sun rose at 9:44 on the morning of November 30, 2018, and when it did, it shined light on a 7.2-magnitude earthquake that had ripped through the area just over an hour earlier. When staff at the Chugiak-Eagle River Library, a branch campus of the Anchorage Public Library, arrived shortly before daybreak, broken windows were already being boarded up by municipal employees working elsewhere in the shared building. Most employees, however, stayed home to assess the damage to their own properties; with no power and many roads impassable, travel which usually took minutes quickly turned into hours. Normal life stopped before it could really begin that Friday as aftershocks were braced for and broken gas and water lines demanded urgent attention.

Alaskans are quite familiar with the earth's extremes, and the state's building regulations are among the most stringent in the United States regarding earthquake preparedness. On Good Friday of 1964, the Great Alaska earthquake rocked the state with a 9.2-magnitude earthquake. The quake lasted a startling 4½ minutes and was followed by tsunamis and building collapses. More than 100 people were killed. After this shocking disaster, building codes were rewritten so that new buildings would be as safe as possible. While many buildings and roads were severely damaged in the 2018 earthquake, there were no deaths and very few injuries. However, the rebuilding process spanned several years and even now continues to affect the Anchorage area. The suburb of Eagle River suffered substantial structural damage, to the extent that two schools have been closed until at least the 2021-22 academic year.

The shared building that now houses the library, the Parks and Recreation Department, and several private businesses was once a grocery store; it is a long, one-story structure. When library and other municipal staff evaluated the condition of their shared building after that morning's earthquake, they saw structural damage in the rear of the building, away from the library. This area was cordoned off

FIGURE 4.5
After the earthquake, Chugiak-Eagle River Branch Library

for everyone's safety until appropriate officials could investigate the entire building more thoroughly, but it did not appear to be a concern for the library. Staff went into the space to take photos and document the disorder caused by tens of thousands of items which had fallen from shelves (figure 4.5). Ceiling tiles had broken and fallen, there were cracks in the sheetrock walls, and a thick layer of dust covered everything. It took some time to coordinate with the relevant local, state, and federal officials to examine the space, as schools and other essential buildings were prioritized ahead of the library. The building was yellow-carded, which meant that only staff members who chose to could enter the space, and personal protective equipment (safety glasses, face masks, helmets, etc.) was required. The dust coating everything was gritty and probably contained volcanic ash, so care was needed to clean it off.

While aftershocks were still a concern and ceiling tiles continued to fall as they were disrupted, risk management officials walked through the library over the course of the day and in the weeks afterward. The library's phones were inundated with so many calls from volunteers offering to help that the staff stopped taking calls altogether; with the yellow card classification, external volunteers could not be allowed inside the building. While the library was closed, FEMA officials, brought in and organized by the local government, and other risk management agents toured the space multiple times; the library manager, Nancy Clark, was in charge of walking them through the damage and explaining the services that staff were unable to provide during recovery. All library services were paused, and patrons were redirected to other branches of the Anchorage Public Library. Almost all of the library's 80,000-item collection was on the floor, and it took a great deal of effort to organize everything and reshelve it correctly; only about 50 items were permanently removed from the collection because of damage from the earthquake. The staff reshelved and cleaned items while working from the back of the space to the front, in a conscious effort to allow outsiders looking through windows to see the chaos and understand why the library was still closed weeks after the earthquake, when most library locations had reopened by the Tuesday after the Friday earthquake. Books that had been checked out prior to the earthquake were returned to other branch libraries for safekeeping, and they were returned to Eagle River after the materials at the library had been reshelved. Once the building was deemed safe, volunteers were allowed in to help with the cleaning. Photographs of the library taken immediately after the earthquake were posted on windows to further elicit compassion among patrons who longed for the library to reopen. Information and updates were also shared on the library's website and social media pages, and local journalists frequently reported on the recovery progress.

The Chugiak-Eagle River Library reopened exactly three weeks after the 7.2-magnitude earthquake when it was reclassified as a green card building. When it did reopen, staff were prepared to teach patrons who had deep, generational connections to the library about the damage and the recovery process: they had prepared a small, interactive exhibit in the front of the space for people to view photographs of the aftermath and write down their own experiences. The community was extremely compassionate, since they had been dealing with their own recovery processes as well. There were still hints of what the community had endured in the many missing ceiling tiles that could not be replaced due to lack of availability. In the weeks and months after the earthquake, inspectors and health and safety officials continued to evaluate the library and the rest of the shared building, but overall, life had returned—mostly—to normal.

The feeling would not last. On May 10, 2019, less than six months after the earthquake, the library was forced to close again when a building inspector found additional structural damage in the rear of the building. Library staff were notified at one o'clock in the afternoon that the building was to be empty by five that evening. It was unclear how long the library would be closed, and staff were dispersed to other branch libraries. Books on hold were sent to other branch libraries for patrons to pick up, websites and social media pages were updated, and other last-minute tasks were completed as they arose. During the closure, Manager Nancy Clark bounced from branch to branch to keep in touch with her staff. Mobile offices had been constructed in the parking lot during the three weeks the library was closed immediately after the earthquake, but just as they were ready to be occupied, the library had reopened and the mobile offices were left empty. This time around, they were occupied by remaining staff trying to continue some form of service during the indefinite closure; it was summer, and the library's busiest season. After a month, the newly discovered damage was addressed and the library was able to reopen on June 11, 2019—and stay open.

Although the library did have a disaster plan prior to the earthquake, it did not include much detail and was therefore not as helpful as it could have been. Nancy Clark noted that it is helpful to take notes during a disaster recovery process, when doing so is possible, to capture granular details that can be extremely helpful in handling a future disaster but which may be quickly forgotten in the immediate aftermath. The existing plan had focused most of its attention on what should be done during the event itself and less on what should happen afterward, whereas an effective document would have been much more comprehensive. It is important to consider an order of operations when evaluating damage from a disaster: should staff enter the building to assess the situation on their own, or wait for first responders or government officials? In the case of an earthquake, when an aftershock could be only a moment away and structural damage may be hidden, the staff should remain at home or a safe distance away from the building until building inspectors can determine if the building is stable. Furthermore, it may be beneficial to have health and safety officials investigate the space to determine what protective equipment may be necessary once reentry is allowed. This guidance should be written into a disaster plan for every kind of event so that when a disaster occurs, the information is readily available.

During the first three-week closure while library staff were reshelving and cleaning, building inspectors, health and safety officials, FEMA agents, and other relevant professionals were constantly going in and out of the building. The staff tried to monitor who was in the library at any given time if an aftershock necessitated an evacuation, but this was difficult because external officials typically did not report their presence to a librarian. Communication was difficult to coordinate between the library, the local government, and FEMA representatives; when crafting a disaster plan, it may help to consider how to establish effective communication practices in order to alleviate this type of frustration after a disaster occurs. When the library was forced to close again several months after the earthquake, it was impossible to handle everything necessary in the few hours allotted: canceling or redirecting periodical subscriptions, deliveries, and mail; closing the book drop; notifying patrons via social media and the library website; determining where staff would go during the closure, and so on. Including in a disaster plan a checklist of tasks to complete if the library must close quickly is strongly encouraged. The best policy is one in which many possible circumstances are thought of and planned out so that the time immediately following a disaster can be used effectively and to the library's best advantage.

Resources for Earthquake Planning

The U.S. Geological Survey (www.usgs.gov) is the only scientific agency in the Department of the Interior. The USGS conducts research on ecosystems, environmental health, natural hazards, groundwater, and climate change. It provides an extensive list of resources and links on the "Earthquake Hazards–Prepare" section of its website (www.usgs.gov/natural-hazards/earthquake-hazards/science/prepare?qt-science_center_objects=0#qt-science_center_objects). The topics range from handbooks on "putting down roots in earthquake country" to a public-domain shakeout procedure ("Drop! Cover! Hold On!") graphic which could easily be posted in the library. There are also an extensive list of "Preparedness Information and Response Agencies," materials in a variety of languages, and resources targeted regionally and by audience (e.g., college students, kids' resources, urban centers, etc.). The site also provides state-specific earthquake, fault, and seismicity information with links to additional state resources (www.usgs.gov/natural-hazards/earthquake-hazards/information-region).

The Earthquake Country Alliance at the University of Southern California (www.earthquakecountry.org/) offers a variety of great resources in a number of languages. One such resource outlines seven steps for earthquake preparation and response. Steps 1 through 4 cover preparation for before an earthquake strikes, while steps 5 and 6 provide instruction for what to do during the event, and the last step explains what to do after the earthquake has struck. These are summarized in a one-page PDF that could easily be printed and posted, or linked to on a library's website (www.earthquakecountry.org/library/Seven_Steps_Flyers_English.pdf).

Fires

Fires can be natural or man-made, or ascribed to mechanical failures or malfunctions, which might not fall firmly into either category. The field report in this section describes a middle-school library that was destroyed by a fire which originated in an electrical room that doubled as a storage closet. No matter how the fire starts, its effect on a library will still be dramatic, and possibly catastrophic.

The frequency and strength of wildfires has increased incredibly over the past few decades. So much so that in its strategic plan (2018; before the notorious Camp Fire), the California Department of Forestry and Fire Protection described the concept of the "fire season" as rendered obsolete by climate change, given that wildfires in the state now occur year-round.

The Camp Fire, which occurred in Butte County in northern California in 2018, spread to more than 150,000 acres total, with the first 100,000 acres affected in just two days. The fire left 85 people dead, destroyed close to 19,000 buildings (almost 14,000 of which were homes), and forced tens of thousands of people to evacuate. During the Camp Fire, the town of Paradise burned down in just four hours. Remarkably, if not providentially, the Paradise library was spared; it was one of the only remaining buildings in town, though it did suffer smoke damage. Five of the library's twenty-six workers lost their homes (Inklebarger 2018). Thanks to help with cleaning and donations, the library was able to open just eight months later in August 2019 (Anderaos 2019).

Libraries across California have shown remarkable resilience and courage in the wake of the state's frequent wildfires. There are countless examples of library workers providing the kind of support that communities can use during the year-round crises. Libraries throughout the state act as information centers, computer hubs, and spaces where displaced residents can contact insurance agencies, FEMA, and worried friends and family.

While it is difficult if not impossible to "fireproof" a facility, there are some preventive measures which can help. Some measures, like creating firebreaks or removing trees, occur outside of the building, and some occur within the facility. These include ensuring that there are functioning smoke detectors on every level, removing any dead tree limbs and keeping gutters clear, and closing or covering all vents, doors, and windows if the building does have to be evacuated. Regular tours or facility inspections can also help to ensure there aren't compromised power cords and such.

The Harvest Park Middle School experienced a fire that caused extensive damage, as described in the next field report.

Field Report from Pleasanton, California: Harvest Park Middle School

THE HARVEST PARK Middle School in Pleasanton, California, was in the midst of its summer vacation in 2018 when a fire broke out in the school's library on the night of Tuesday, July 3. The fire originated in a rear electrical room doubling as a storage closet, and quickly spread throughout the library. The local fire department was summoned automatically when the building's fire alarms were triggered, but firefighters had to wait to be given access to the campus by an administrator. Approximately thirty minutes after they first arrived, firefighters extinguished the fire, but there was significant damage to the ceiling and the attic space above it (figure 4.6). When Susan King, the library's media tech and sole staff member, arrived the next morning along with the principal and superintendent, they could smell that everything in the library—carpet, walls, ceiling tiles, books, furniture—had sustained smoke damage, and much of it was also water damaged. The textbooks in storage that were being saved for the upcoming school year had also sustained smoke damage. And upon further examination, the integrity of the entire roof was found to be compromised.

The library was insured with a district-wide policy that paid for building repairs and the replacement of furniture, fixtures, books, and equipment. ATI Restoration, based in Anaheim, California, was quickly hired by the insurance company to lead the recovery effort; a manager was assigned to supervise the work crew and was always reachable by school administrators or librarians if any questions arose, which facilitated communication between school representatives and the company. ATI staff recorded and photographed everything that was taken to be de-smoked: books, couches, tables, chairs, and technological equipment. The de-smoking process took several months, but ATI asked King to make a list of materials to prioritize.

FIGURE 4.6
Harvest Park Middle School interior

In the meantime, a very small, temporary library had been set up in a classroom by the beginning of the school year and was used for the first month of the semester. A longer-term interim library was created out of a quadruple portable classroom that was open by October; in that space students could read and study during lunch and before or after school, but there were no books for them to borrow. During the school year, e-mails were regularly sent out to the school's staff, and teachers talked to their students about the library's recovery. School administrators were responsible for sharing information with students' families and the public, and did so via e-mail, the school website, and the school's social media sites (Facebook and Instagram). Staff at the Pleasanton Unified School District used their website and local newspaper to also share news of the library's progress. These two levels of information providers—school administrators and the district—reflect the two levels of stakeholders in charge of the recovery process. The district took charge of interacting with insurance representatives, the city of Pleasanton, and the state of California to initiate and move the recovery process along. School administrators met with architects, contractors, and district representatives to guide the process, and King identified what was needed by researching the values of destroyed furniture, equipment, and books (the cost of replacing books alone was $78,000).

The community was incredibly supportive throughout the recovery process, but especially when the library was relocating and constantly unpacking and organizing books; student volunteers helped unbox and sort books every week, and libraries throughout the school district loaned their book carts. While students could not borrow books, King and a group of parent volunteers organized a book swap for students, with materials donated by the school staff and families. Small grants were awarded by the Parent Teacher Student Association for the purchase of tables and stools, and parent donations supported the purchase of new chairs, step stools, and artwork for the library. Teachers suggested books and research materials the library could purchase, and one of the district's elementary schools provided a set of encyclopedias and other elementary-level reference books for English-learning students.

In October, three months after the fire, the first of many truckloads of restored and de-smoked books began arriving. Each truckload was full of boxes, which contained between 5 and 10 books nestled in protective packing paper. The first books King had directed restorers to prioritize—based upon demand and the available space in the interim one-classroom library—were from the fiction section, but there were not enough shelves to hold these books in that temporary space. So instead, books were sorted and lined up in rows on the floor and on library carts that had been borrowed from other libraries in the school district. Once the portable classroom was delivered to the Harvest Park campus and appropriately reinforced to bear the weight of full bookshelves, the school library's surviving wall-mounted shelves were moved to that facility. The portable facility was soon filled with shelves, and the library relocated there. When the majority of the fiction section books had been de-smoked, students were able to borrow materials again. Gradually, more books and furniture were returned to the library after being restored, and new books were purchased as insurance funding was received.

Establishing the temporary library by the beginning of the school year was the chief priority for King and school administrators. Once the interim library was ready for students and books were able to be checked out by mid-October, the next priority was to address the needs of the real library. Throughout the fall, a team of architects met with the district's project manager, King, and the school principal to decide how the space would be rebuilt; insurance funding would only cover replacing what had been destroyed rather than a complete renovation. However, there were still changes to be considered: accessibility requirements, moving the HVAC system from the roof to a maintenance room or on the grounds outside, repurposing the electrical room where the fire started, and so on. The approval process for the plan, which required agreement from both the Pleasanton Unified School District and the state of California, took several months. Demolition work began in the summer of 2019, one year after the fire, when the roof, ceiling, some walls and doors, and all surfaces with smoke damage (carpet, ventilation ducts, etc.) were removed. Although the state eventually approved the building plans, the bidding process took longer than expected, and construction could not begin until February 2020.

The construction work was intended to be completed by July 2020, with workdays scheduled from 3:30 p.m. to 10:00 p.m. to avoid noise and safety concerns for students. Unfortunately, only one month into the work, the state announced a shelter-in-place order in mid-March to curb the spread of the coronavirus, and construction stopped for two weeks. After this setback, construction was able to resume after being declared essential, but it continued to be affected by the pandemic as materials and laborers grew increasingly difficult to find. Because students had moved to a remote learning format, construction could take place during normal daytime hours for the remainder of the project. Construction work on the library was done in the summer of 2020, two years after the fire, and shelves, books, and furniture were brought back in from the portable facility, and from where they had been kept in storage. Because of the pandemic, however, the library was not able to open fully for the 2020-21 school year as originally planned; it was not until late September 2020 that all the books were returned from the interim library and organized on shelves. By that time, however, more than two years after the fire, the library was open for students to request and hold books and for librarians to bring them out to a designated pickup area.

Before the 2018 fire, the Pleasanton Unified School District had a disaster plan that laid out who would be contacted and what would be needed to reopen the library. Having this information at the ready was noted by the library's media tech, Susan King, as being very helpful, although she only learned about it as the library progressed in its recovery. The district's project manager was an extremely valuable resource, as this gave King a point of contact for any questions or concerns that arose, as well as a guide throughout the process. She reflected that while it is important to have disaster plans, it is equally important for everyone to know about them and be able to understand what (and how much time) is involved in them. The school district had contact information for an insurance representative and could ask the agent about restoration companies; it knew the process involved in getting a temporary building set up; and it knew enough to expect that it would be quite some time before life would return to normal. The school staff, by contrast, simply followed the lead of the district with few expectations.

In spite of the fire and the main library being closed for two years (and being unable to immediately return to full, in-person service anyway due to the pandemic), King does not believe that her fundamental role as a librarian changed during that time. Rather, the most important thing to her was to foster excitement and interest in reading, and that continued to happen even while making do in the temporary and interim library spaces. The donated book swap in the fall of 2018 allowed students to choose a new (to them) book to keep. Student volunteers were eager each week to help unpack and sort de-smoked and newly purchased books. While the library was closed, King shared book recommendations on the school's social media pages and learned how to create digital book displays. While it was certainly far from ideal to be removed from the permanent library for such an extended period of time, the disaster encouraged staff at the Harvest Park Middle School to think about libraries in new ways.

Resources for Fire Planning

The National Interagency Fire Center (www.nifc.gov/) is comprised of eight agencies and organizations. They support all types of emergency responses, but their main focus is to provide resources for coordinating wildland firefighting. Theirs is a helpful website that offers a wide range of resources, from maps to statistics to a section dedicated to prevention measures, education, and mitigation.

The Illinois Fire Service Institute Library (www.fsi.illinois.edu/content/library/) has a mission to help firefighters and first responders "do their work through training, education, information, and research." While materials lending is restricted to Illinois residents, its website offers helpful tools that can be used by any library, such as a number of LibGuides on fire-related topics. Beyond these resources, you can also check your state for similar state-specific resources.

Floods

FEMA defines flooding as the partial or complete inundation of two or more acres of normally dry land area or of two or more properties. Flooding is a general and temporary condition that results from the following:

- the overflow of tidal or inland water
- the rapid and unusual accumulation or runoff of surface water from any source
- mudflow
- a dam failure or the collapse of land along a lake shore or similar body of water as a result of erosion

According to the World Economic Forum, flooding is the most common natural disaster in terms of occurrence, accounting for close to half of all the natural disasters worldwide. Flooding is often a by-product of other weather-related disasters, such as storm runoff during hurricanes, ice-melts, and so on. As discussed in chapter 5, flooding is also the most common reason for FEMA disaster declarations related to building damage in the United States.

There are steps to consider ahead of time to minimize flood risk. These include keeping drains and gutters clear, and extending downspouts if needed. In colder climates, it means removing ice and snow so that they do not cause dams. Regular roof inspections, preventive landscaping that encourages absorption, not runoff, and vigilance for any type of water stains or signs of leaks or mold can be included in routine building inspections.

According to FEMA, between 2014 and 2018, over 40 percent of flood insurance claims came from outside high-risk flood areas. If it is not already a requirement, you should investigate purchasing flood insurance. For those outside of a floodplain, where the risk is lower, there is often a reduced rate for this insurance. Note that there is typically a thirty-day waiting period from the purchase date until the flood insurance policy goes into effect, so plan accordingly. See www.floodsmart.gov/ for more information on the National Flood Insurance Program, and for links to current flood zone maps. On a community level, you should consider what materials may be necessary for flood response, such as pumps, sandbags, and maybe clay for temporary barriers, along with cleanup kits.

Because sea levels are rising, and flood zone maps are being updated and redrawn, the likelihood of flooding is becoming a greater risk in more and more communities. In Midland, Michigan, the Grace A. Dow Memorial Library experienced extensive flooding in 2020, as described in our next field report.

---------- **Field Report from Midland, Michigan:** ----------
Flooding at the Grace A. Dow Memorial Library

THE MORNING OF Tuesday, May 19, 2020, began like many others in Michigan lately. As a result of the coronavirus pandemic that swept across the United States earlier that spring, many people were working from home or had become unemployed. The Grace A. Dow Memorial Library, the public library serving the city of Midland, had been closed since March 16 due to an executive order passed by the governor, Gretchen Whitmer. It had been raining steadily for several days, and the water threatened to overwhelm two dams in the heart of Michigan. Midland officials were particularly concerned because the dams were only 8 and 30 miles away up the Tittabawassee River, which flows through downtown Midland. Early that Tuesday, residents' cell phones blared with an ominous warning: a dam failure was predicted and people were encouraged to evacuate. Officials disagreed, however, about the validity of the warning, and decided that life would carry on as normal, if a little wet. But late that afternoon, 30 miles northwest of Midland, the Edenville Dam did fail. And because the evacuation warning had been ignored, no one was prepared.

When the news broke of the dam failure, the director of the Grace A. Dow Memorial Library, Miriam Andrus, was standing in the backyard of the library evaluating the water levels. The Dow Memorial Library is a three-story, mid-century, modern-style building with walls of windows and a collection of approximately 200,000 items. The lowest level is mostly underground and houses 80,000 books and other materials for children and young adults, as well as the city's historic newspaper collection, meeting rooms, and mechanical equipment. Behind the library runs Snake Creek, which normally runs only two feet deep; when Andrus arrived late in the afternoon, the creek had already risen dramatically and was mere feet below the windows of the library. Andrus began pulling materials away from windows and walls in the lower level and used a library cell phone with programmed contacts to call the most essential personnel to help. Beyond moving materials, however, it was difficult to know how to prepare the building for a flood. According to the 500-year floodplain map, the library would not flood even in a worst-case scenario, so it was anybody's guess as to what was going to happen. By evening, all the materials close to the windows had been moved and essential staff had returned home to evaluate and better prepare their own homes. Knowing things would get worse before they would get better, Andrus spent the night at the library.

At three o'clock in the morning of Wednesday, May 20, water reached the library. The same essential staff members were called back to move materials again, this time to a higher level. By the time the water stopped rising, the bottoms of the windows were submerged by as much as 11 inches of water, the "weathertight" seals around the window frames began to fail, and the mortar between the bricks was disintegrating. As a result, the lowest level of the building was flooded with 3 to 6 inches of water. To make matters worse, there were predictions that the Sanford Dam, only eight miles from Midland and already overwhelmed before the Edenville Dam's failure, would also collapse and let loose another surge. As the director of a city department, Andrus called her colleagues at the Midland Office of Parks and Recreation and worked with them to build a dam of their own behind the library, bringing in truckloads of dirt to make a barrier taller than the water level. Six industrial-grade pumps were used to drain the building and the yard immediately outside it. By Thursday morning, the water in the library was under control, with the exception of mechanical rooms that remained flooded; because the electrical conduits were threatened, the staff made the decision to shut off a main power breaker to prevent an electrical disaster, but this caused the library to lose phone and internet service. Overall, the building was soaked to its foundation, but the lower level was at least made accessible again.

88 | CHAPTER 4

FIGURE 4.7
Michigan National Guard helps out at the Grace A. Dow Memorial Library

To help begin the recovery process, the Michigan National Guard had been called up by Governor Whitmer, but there was little they could do for residents and local businesses until the water receded. By Thursday, while much of Midland was still under inches or feet of water, the Grace A. Dow Memorial Library was ready for help. Library staff and the Michigan National Guard worked together to remove everything from the building's lower level (figure 4.7). Because the building's elevators were no longer operational, the youth services collection, craft materials, furniture, historic newspapers, and computers all had to be carried up the stairs. Although it was difficult to stress the importance of focusing on the library when houses were being washed away, the library was one of the few buildings that was even accessible so soon after the dam failures, and the National Guard was instrumental in getting everything out quickly. The library's heating and cooling systems, located in the still-flooded mechanical rooms, were damaged, and rising humidity was a fast-approaching threat in the warmth of springtime (figure 4.8).

In total, the library lost about 500 items as a result of the flooding. The damage to the building, however, was far more extensive. Midland County applied for FEMA relief to fund up to three-quarters of the area's recovery, which the city supplemented with insurance payouts. Disaster recovery vendors were called in all over the city to help the local hospital, university, arts center, and so on. The library hired the well-known restoration company ServPro to remove drywall and

FIGURE 4.8
Grace A. Dow Memorial Library HVAC systems

other building materials that had gotten wet, install temporary industrial dehumidifiers and drying machines, and disinfect all surfaces that had been contaminated by the dirty floodwater. Library and Parks and Recreation staff removed carpeting and did much of the other labor themselves, and the flooded lower level had been dried out by Saturday, May 23, only four days after the disaster.

Because the library had been closed since March, there was no continuity of service to uphold during recovery efforts. However, it was still vital to inform the Midland community about how the library was dealing with the flood. The library has a large presence in Midland, and it was important for patrons to feel involved in its recovery even when they were unable to volunteer their time or services themselves; not only were they recovering their own properties and businesses, but distancing precautions to prevent the spread of the coronavirus were still in effect, and the library was unable to take advantage of the normal ready supply of volunteers. Information was shared to three key resources: the city website, local newspapers, and the library's social media channels. Immediately, press releases were published on the city website and in local newspapers. These resources also shared information about other impacted services, making them useful places for residents who were looking to understand the flood's toll on the city. Before recovery work started and continuing throughout the process, library staff posted videos and updates to the Dow Memorial Library's Facebook page. By sharing the process virtually, library staff allowed patrons to feel involved and informed, as well as eliciting compassion from those who eagerly awaited the resumption of library services. Some semblance of normal service returned in early July, just less than two months after the flood, when the library began to offer curbside pickup for patrons who requested materials in advance. This distanced format of delivery became common during the pandemic and was the new "normal" of the time.

Before the flood on May 19, 2020, the Grace A. Dow Memorial Library did not have a disaster plan. After this emergency, Director Miriam Andrus now intends to create one, and is confident that her experience will lead to a more comprehensive policy. In thinking retrospectively about the flood and how it could impact the library's future disaster response, Andrus has come to recognize several important elements to include or consider when writing a disaster plan. Perhaps the most important components in any plan are accurate contact information for all library staff and building maintenance professionals, and a schedule for verifying or updating that information as necessary. The contacts document should be readily accessible at any time, both in the library and off-site, so that it can be retrieved immediately upon learning of an emergency. Physical and digital copies of the plan should exist on personal computers, library servers, personal or library mobile phones, and off-site as well. Contact information for volunteer groups can also be a valuable resource when creating an information dissemination plan (i.e., a phone tree).

It is also important to know the limitations of one's staff. During an emergency, people experience chaos, panic, fear, stress, and other overwhelming emotions. The essential staff responsible for responding immediately to a disaster should be chosen carefully, and one factor should be their ability to handle stressful situations. Burnout is a very real concern when so many things require immediate attention, and a library director or writer of a disaster plan should understand the strengths and weaknesses of individual staff members. In the case of the Dow Library, Andrus was in the library for almost four straight days and only had time for brief naps; some members of the staff may be unwilling or unable to do that, and it is best to be prepared for such an obstacle in advance. (Consider, also, if someone may be forced to spend a night in the library, and if there is adequate space or even a blanket for them.) You should note which members of the staff are capable of lifting or moving things, and which are good with children or can maintain a calm façade, and then tailor the policy to take advantage of people's strengths and protect them from their weaknesses.

Finally, a thorough disaster plan should include a policy or guidelines for how the staff should protect patrons if an emergency happens during open hours. Although the flood occurred during what would have been business hours on a weekday, the library was luckily (if one chooses to think positively) closed due to another form of disaster: the coronavirus pandemic. However, if patrons are in the building during a flash flood, tornado, or other dangerous situation, the staff should be prepared to keep them as safe and calm as possible. You should try to use specific language that will convey authority but not cause panic; provide distracting activities for children if there is to be a period of sheltering in place; and schedule fire drills, first aid workshops, and other preparatory experiences for staff. A disaster response can be accomplished on the fly as a catastrophe strikes, but having a plan prepared ahead of time can help reduce stress and improve the response to what can be a truly overwhelming situation. Even though the unexpected may never happen, having clear steps to follow and information at hand when it is needed can help staff respond and keep people safe when disaster occurs.

Resources for Flood Planning

Many of the resources for other weather-related disasters cover flooding, especially those that address hurricane preparedness. The USGS offers the Flood Inundation Mapper (https://fim.wim.usgs.gov/fim/), which provides sets of maps that show streamflow conditions, and forecasts where flooding would occur under selected conditions. This tool could be a great conversation starter, since it helps communities visualize potential flooding scenarios before they happen. Historical flood information is included, as well as potential loss estimates based on flood severity.

The National Weather Service also offers a range of flood resources, and provides social media graphics for easy alerts (www.weather.gov/dvn/Awareness_Weeks#Top). FEMA offers a wide range of resources related to flood prevention and mitigation, flood insurance, and flood zone determination. A handy tool to get started with flood risk assessment is from FEMA's flood map service center (https://msc.fema.gov/portal/home), which offers the capability of entering an address to determine an area's flood risk.

Though not specific to flooding, the National Council of State Housing Agencies offers information on emergency housing assistance (www.ncsha.org/emergency-housing-assistance/), including emergency rental assistance programs by state.

The focus of this chapter was on natural and weather-related disasters, which are statistically the most likely type of disaster a library will encounter. Each library needs to assess its risks based on a variety of factors, with the potential that two libraries just miles apart with identical hurricane risks might have very different plans if, for example, one is most at risk of flooding and the other is primarily at risk of wind damage. Yet, the three main takeaways from this chapter apply to virtually all libraries: the most likely natural disaster risks are somewhat predictable, the risks of weather-related disasters have increased markedly in recent years, and there are excellent resources, particularly from the federal government, to assess and plan for such disasters. Given the plethora of tools and support systems for learning about these, planning for such events could be an easy way to involve the community in interacting around the subject of disaster preparedness.

REFERENCES

Anderaos, Deb. 2019. "Paradise Branch Library Reopens following Camp Fire." *Action News Now*, Chico, CA. www.actionnewsnow.com/content/news/Paradise-Branch-Library-reopened-Thursday-513522291.html.

Federal Emergency Management Agency. 2011. "Definitions." www.fema.gov/pdf/nfip/manual201205/content/22_definitions.pdf.

———. 2021. "What Is a Flood Map?" www.floodsmart.gov/flood-map-zone/about.

Ferraro, Paul. 2018. "Start Preparing for the Next Hurricane Irma." *Johns Hopkins Engineering*, Summer, 44.

Fountain, Henry. 2021. "2020 Ties 2016 as Hottest Yet, European Analysis Says." *New York Times*, January 8. www.nytimes.com/2021/01/08/climate/hottest-year-ever.html?action=click&module=Well&pgtype=Homepage&section=Climate%20and%20Environment.

Gaul, Gilbert M. 2019. *Geography of Risk: Epic Storms, Rising Seas, and the Cost of America's coasts.* New York: Sarah Crichton Books.

Inklebarger, Timothy. 2018. "California Libraries in Wildfires' Wake: Paradise, Other Communities with Disaster." *American Libraries,* November 16. https://americanlibrariesmagazine.org/blogs/the-scoop/california-libraries-in-wildfires-wake/.

LaFaro, Alyssa. 2021. "Building Resilience for Storm-Battered NC." *The Well*, February 2. University of North Carolina at Chapel Hill. https://thewell.unc.edu/2021/02/02/building-resilience-for-storm-battered-n-c/.

Miller, Annetta. 2005. "Sierra Leonean Proverb." *African Wisdom for Life.* Nairobi, Kenya: Paulines Publications Africa.

National Oceanic and Atmospheric Administration, National Hurricane Center and Central Pacific Hurricane Center. 2021. "Saffir-Simpson Hurricane Wind Scale." www.nhc.noaa.gov/aboutsshws.php.

National Weather Service. 2021. "Taking Shelter from the Storm." www.weather.gov/safety/tornado-prepare.

State of California, CAL Fire. 2018. "Strategic Plan." www.fire.ca.gov/about-us/strategic-plan/.

U.S. Geological Survey. "Modified Mercalli Intensity Scale." www.usgs.gov/media/images/modified-mercalli-intensity-scale.

———. "The Science of Earthquakes." 2021. www.usgs.gov/natural-hazards/earthquake-hazards/science/science-earthquakes?qt-science_center_objects=0#qt-science_center_objects.

World Economic Forum. 2016. "Which Natural Disasters Hit Most Frequently." www.weforum.org/agenda/2016/01/which-natural-disasters-hit-most-frequently/.

CHAPTER 5

Physical Facilities

*In the moment of crisis, the wise build bridges
and the foolish build dams.*

—*Nigerian proverb*

EVERY LIBRARY FACILITY, BRAND-NEW OR HISTORIC, HAS UNIQUE CHARACTERISTICS and challenges, and while most think of major natural disasters like wildfires or hurricanes when they consider disaster planning and emergency management, ongoing maintenance is also an integral part of disaster preparedness and mitigation. Small-scale disasters resulting from maintenance failures and unforeseen mishaps occur much more frequently than large-scale, catastrophic disasters.

Even minor incidents, like a tree that falls in a rainstorm and damages the roof, allowing water to pour onto the stacks, can be very costly in terms of time and resources. The routine inspection of library facilities for maintenance issues can help reduce not only the frequency but also the severity of such incidents. With regular vigilance, it may be possible to prevent problems from happening. Not every part of the facility will need the same level of surveillance. A discussion with the facility's management team or maintenance department, and open channels of communication can help you keep up-to-date on predictable issues such as leaking pipes or heating system malfunctions. The facility team's feedback, along with systematic assessment, can illuminate the age, condition, and idiosyncrasies of various parts of the facility, and point to areas that may be problematic or that signal emerging problems.

Roughly speaking, the facility maintenance and preparations related to disaster planning fall into four categories:

1. Is the building situated or structured in ways that increase or exacerbate certain susceptibilities? This was largely determined when the site was selected, and the building constructed. Such an assessment will inform the team about the likelihood or floods or fires, rather than allowing for changes in the likelihood of them occurring.

| 93

2. Are the building's internal systems (electrical, plumbing, security) maintained or optimal for minimizing adverse consequences during a disaster?
3. Are the human and social aspects of your building plan (insurance policies in place, who will ensure the doors are closed and circuit-breakers are shut off in specific scenarios) appropriate, understood, and in place?
4. Are the daily and regular procedures (shutting off lights at the end of the day, monthly tests of smoke alarms) that should be done actually being performed as expected?

Note that unlike many other aspects of disaster planning, the first two items, which are perhaps the most important ones, are completely beyond the purview and control of most librarians and their staff. Thus, assessing and preparing your building to minimize disaster risks requires, to some extent, engagement with outside professionals. This chapter attempts to outline ways to help engage with such professionals, and to help leverage their skills for a more physically resilient organization.

Inspections

Regularly scheduled building inspections of the interior and exterior parts of the building on a daily, monthly, quarterly, or annual basis can help with disaster prevention. For most libraries in a town or university, there are maintenance professionals who can advise you, and once the necessary procedures have been outlined, many of these inspections can be handled by library staff. For others, you can invite your insurance agent for a tour of the facility (some agents actually conduct routine, unannounced inspections) and ask for feedback. When your favorite and trusted electrician is coming to do a project, perhaps you can ask to schedule an extra thirty minutes for them to walk through the building to see if anything triggers concern. Often these experts can identify very easy-to-fix issues that may not be visible to you and your staff. For instance, at one public library they had installed state-of-the-art fire doors between two sections of the building, the main part and the community room. Between these sections, there were also restrooms. To make egress to the restrooms easier, library workers kept the fire doors propped open. When the routine insurance inspection was completed, the company immediately notified the director and the doors now remain closed, serving their important purpose of protecting against and reducing the spread of smoke or fire.

A regular review of insurance policies can help ensure adequate coverage; for instance, are the building *and* collections covered for damage? Different types of materials may need different types of coverage. Do you know the procedures to follow if a disaster occurs; for example, can you begin salvaging items before an insurance adjuster visits? Do you know how to file a claim? Do you have a print copy of the insurance policy and the agent's contact information stored off-site? Knowing these things ahead of time can help save time, reduce stress, and streamline any recovery processes that may need to take place.

Tables 5.1 through 5.3 provide templates for interior and exterior building inspections to ensure regular, ongoing attention to the physical facility. These templates can easily be adapted and scaled up or down to adjust for a specific facility.

TABLE 5.1
Sample interior building inspection schedule

AREA	INSPECTED BY			FREQUENCY
	Fire Dept.	Staff	Service/Contract	
Interior of building	X			annually
		X		daily
Smoke detectors		X		monthly
Fire extinguishers		X		monthly
			X	annually
Fire drills		X		quarterly
Furnace cleaning			X	annually
Air conditioning			X	annually
Electrical cords		X		monthly
Boiler			X	annually
Disaster supplies		X		monthly

TABLE 5.2
Sample interior building inspection assessment

AREA	Acceptable Yes	Acceptable No	ACTION REQUIRED	COMPLETED (DATE)
Foyers:				
Lights/Switches				
Obstructions				
Housekeeping				
Signs				
Community Room:				
Lights/Switches				
Windows				
Fire extinguisher				
Housekeeping				
Adult Section:				
Lights/Switches				
Windows				
Fire extinguisher				
Computer Area				
Computer room:				
Lights/Switches				
Windows				
Fire extinguisher				
Housekeeping				

TABLE 5.3
Sample exterior building inspection assessment

AREA	Acceptable Yes	Acceptable No	ACTION REQUIRED	COMPLETED (DATE)
Building obstruction:				
Drainpipes for A/C				
Roof:				
Loose shingles				
Debris				
Drainpipes				
Gutters				
Windows:				
Wells				
Debris				
Fire exits				
Drainage:				
Basement exit				
Landscaping:				
Tree branches, limbs				
Shrubbery				
Obstructions				

These tables can be adapted and integrated into the library's disaster plan, along with a simple blueprint that identifies the locations of emergency exits, fire alarms, smoke sensors, fire extinguishers, shut-off valves, and power switches.

Other information relating to the physical facility to include in the disaster plan are the following:

- Written description, with a diagram, of the locations of power switches, shut-off valves, and fire extinguishers
- List of locations with whom the plan has been shared (e.g., Fire Department)

- Areas in the facility where flammable or noxious materials are stored
- Clear instructions for deactivating any alarm systems
- Fire plan
- Written evacuation procedures (daytime, evening, and weekend)
- Clear instructions for dealing with a bomb threat
- How to deal with rodents, insects, and mold
- Procedures for dealing with vandalism
- Procedures for structural accidents (e.g., collapse of shelving)
- List of salvage priorities
- Salvage plan and procedures
- Resource list of supplies, vendors

For the first four items in the above list, simple descriptions or explanations can be included in the plan. For the remainder of the list, the templates in the sections below can be adapted for inclusion as needed.

Fire Plan

The fire plan should be clearly posted and regularly reviewed. It can be as simple as these four steps:

1. Upon detection of fire or smoke, the staff member should go to the nearest telephone and use the intercom function to page all the phone stations in the building.
2. Announce the fire or smoke and its location, and alert all staff to begin evacuation procedures.
3. Call the Fire Department—include the local direct number here if applicable.
4. If the fire is small, such as in a wastebasket, staff can decide whether to put it out with a fire extinguisher, following the instructions on the canister.

You should offer library workers regular training on fire preparedness. Invite the local fire chief (or equivalent) for a day of demonstrations and practice with fire extinguishers; the chief can also offer guidance on judging when it is appropriate to use them. Regular training and drills can help ensure that staff know what to do ahead of time; familiarity with procedures not only saves time, but can also save lives.

Evacuation Procedures

Every facility should have clearly posted instructions for emergency evacuation procedures, along with regularly scheduled drills to practice those procedures. The evacuation procedures document should include a designated meeting place for library workers and patrons. Some libraries use sign-in mechanisms or scheduling software so that it is easy to identify who is in the building at any given time; this can help make certain that everyone is accounted for in the event of an emergency that requires evacuation.

The procedures should include adaptations that can be tailored to different conditions, such as the time of day or if the fire evacuation process differs from a bomb threat evacuation process. The text box (below) is a sample of simple evacuation procedures for a small public library, which can be readily adapted for other facilities. Note that the key points can be capitalized or stated in bold, or in a different-colored font for emphasis and easy referral.

---------- **Sample: Daytime Emergency Evacuation Procedures** ----------

The DESIGNATED MEETING PLACE is the PIONEER CEMETERY located next to the Library.

1. **CIRCULATION and INFORMATION DESK WORKERS:**
   These staff will check the SEATING AREA, the PUBLIC ACCESS COMPUTER ROOM, the QUIET ROOM, ADULT STACKS AREA, PUBLIC RESTROOMS, and COMMUNITY ROOM for PATRONS.

   Any PATRONS in these areas should be directed to leave the building immediately and gather in the DESIGNATED MEETING PLACE.

   The LIBRARY WORKERS should evacuate the building and go to the DESIGNATED MEETING PLACE.

2. **COMMUNICATION CENTER and OFFICE WORKERS:**
   OFFICE WORKERS will check the CHILDREN'S AREA, the YOUNG ADULT AREA, and the CHILDREN'S RESTROOM. Any PATRONS in these areas should be directed to immediately leave the building and gather in the DESIGNATED MEETING PLACE.

   The ADMINISTRATIVE ASSISTANT or DESIGNATE will collect the STAFF SIGN-IN SHEET and EVACUATE the building. Go to the DESIGNATED MEETING PLACE.

3. **DOWNSTAIRS:**
    The ASSISTANT DIRECTOR or DESIGNATE should check for any WORKERS in the downstairs LOUNGE and STAFF RESTROOM for anyone present and direct them to the nearest exit. Go to the DESIGNATED MEETING PLACE.

    If fire or other circumstances prevent Downstairs people from using the stairs to the side door exit, staff should direct patrons through the EMERGENCY EXIT WINDOWS in the STAFF LOUNGE.

For EVENING and WEEKENDS: Depending on where the emergency is located, one worker should check downstairs and through the children's area, and one should check the upstairs area. Ask patrons to leave according to daytime evacuation procedures.

Note: Inasmuch as they can, workers should get into the habit of relating where they will be when they leave their work area; this small effort may prove to be life-saving in an emergency. Regular practice and drills will serve to commit the routine steps to memory, so that in the case of a true emergency, response will be more fluid and automatic.

For any type of evacuation or fire emergency, the acronym RACE can serve as an apt reminder of the steps to take:

R = Remove anyone from immediate danger
A = Activate the alarm system, and call 911
C = Confine the fire, and close all doors and windows
E = Evacuate (and *if* it can be done safely, extinguish the fire)

Bomb Threat Procedures

In the event of a bomb threat, clearly spelled-out procedures can help guide the staff to act logically and appropriately. The following steps are guidelines that can be adapted to any disaster plan:

1. If a suspicious object or package is found, notify the library administration and police at once.
2. If a phone call is received that reports a bomb, the staff member receiving the call should remain calm and try to get answers to the following questions if at all possible:
    a. When will the bomb explode?
    b. Where is the bomb?
    c. When was it planted?
    d. What does the bomb look like?
    e. What type of bomb is it?

3. The staff member receiving the threat should carefully note the following:
    a. The exact words used by the caller
    b. Any explicit motive for the threat
    c. The quality of the caller's voice. Do they sound young or old, or have any distinguishing vocal characteristics? Do they sound nervous, determined, and so on? While these determinations may seem subjective, they may help the police in their efforts.
4. While on the phone, the staff member should write a note for a nearby employee and have them notify the police. That employee should also notify all other appropriate individuals, including the director.
5. Once the director has been informed of the threat, the building should be evacuated according to the emergency evacuation instructions.
6. The police or a comparable agency will determine when the building is safe for reentry.

Other Considerations

More mundane issues, such as how to deal with pests and conditions (e.g., rodents, insects, and mold) that might emerge as a result of a disaster, should be decided upon at the local level and included in the disaster plan. For instance, is there a local exterminator the library will employ? What about the safety of their chemical products for library materials and humans?

As a result of reduced occupancy during the COVID-19 pandemic, Mediterranean recluse spiders were found in the basements of some University of Michigan buildings, including the library, in early 2021. The spiders were discovered by the university's Pest Management Department as a result of routine inspections in late January. Although bites from this type of spider are extremely rare, upon learning of the spiders, the library management closed the facility. They later apologized for any alarm and inconvenience the closure may have caused.

According to the university spokesperson, Kim Broekhuizen: "A misunderstanding of the situation led the library to close for two days. Based on what we all know now, library managers agree that it was a mistake to close the building and they apologize for the inconvenience to the university community." The university's Pest Management team continues to monitor and treat for the arachnid intruders, and now has safety precautions for anyone working in areas where the spiders have been found. These precautions include wearing a hat, gloves, a long-sleeved shirt, and close-toed boots or shoes when handling any items that have been stored, such as boxes, lumber, or rocks (Quinlan 2021).

A well spelled-out section on procedures for dealing with vandalism and one for structural accidents (e.g., collapse of shelving) that are tailored to the individual library will round out the physical facilities section of the plan. These do not need to be extensive prescriptions; a half-page or one-page description of immediate response procedures can be adequate. The disaster plan should be shared with the local fire and police departments, the town/village/city office, the insurance carrier, and the library system or regional headquarters, if the library is a consortium member. Electronic and print copies of the plan should also be housed at the library's main desk, at the director or manager's home, and at the board president's (or equivalent) home.

When it comes to buildings and disaster preparedness, there are doubtless many examples where a "stitch in time might have saved nine" or "an ounce of prevention might have been worth a pound of cure." One of the most dramatic examples of this is the Burton Barr Central Library in Phoenix, Arizona. In 2017, the library experienced catastrophic flooding that could have been prevented. A report from the city attorney showed that repeated warnings by building inspectors of leaks and corrosion in the sprinkler systems were largely ignored, for many years. When the system did malfunction, severe flooding occurred, with 6,000 volumes damaged and an estimate of $10,000,000 in repair costs. As a result of the egregious oversight, three city employees were fired, two were demoted, and one was suspended (Boehm 2017).

Salvage

Knowing ahead of time what and where the most highly valued items are can help immensely in terms of immediate response and recovery efforts. Salvage priorities should be included in the disaster plan, with clear descriptions of where the items are located in the library. These will be different for each library, and will differ in each library setting. The Northeast Document Conservation Center provides guidelines for the difficult task of prioritizing items at www.nedcc.org/preservation101/session-8/8preparing-for-disaster. The center also provides access to a number of free resources for help with disaster response and recovery, including salvage guidelines for a variety of materials: www.nedcc.org/free-resources/disaster-assistance/. Besides priorities, specific plans for salvage procedures for your setting should also be included in the disaster plan, as well as a resource list that is specific to your organization.

State libraries often offer guidance and resources on these topics, such as the Alaska State Libraries, Archives and Museums (https://lam.alaska.gov/disaster

_resources). Their website links to extensive resources for disaster preparedness, including salvage concerns. The New Jersey State Library has an extensive list of resources for salvaging library materials (www.njstatelib.org/services_for_libraries/resources/disaster_planning/salvage/) which could be used in disaster plans. If you find that you need assistance for small-scale disasters at your library, you may be able to consult local or state-level preservation organizations. These organizations may offer limited funds up to a few thousand dollars for disaster response.

---------- **All in a Day's Work** ----------

FOR A PERIOD of six years, the author was a public library director. Over the course of that time, there were regularly seemingly minor (and some not so minor) building issues to deal with, all in the course of a day's work.

As soon as I took on the director position, I discovered that my knowledge of the inner workings of a library had to extend to basic knowledge of facility concerns, like plumbing, shut-off valves, how to reset thermostats after power outages, and how and when to turn off the outdoor water fountain in the wintertime. The library facility had recently been renovated, but after that renovation, and concomitant with my hiring, the facility became independent and autonomous, meaning that the village relinquished any physical support, although the village engineer was still available for assistance and consultation. He was a valuable informational resource and support.

In my second week as director, we had what we thought was a minor leak in the exit area near our Community Room. After intense summer thunderstorms, water was coming through the ceiling tiles in the hallway; this also happened to be where the air conditioning (A/C) unit was located. We contacted the company which had installed the unit, and they came to assess. They assured us the leak had nothing to do with the A/C unit, and that the storms were responsible for the water leakage. So we replaced the ceiling tiles and didn't give it much more thought.

A few days later, a patron reported that water was pouring down the back wall of the women's restroom. Given that we had experienced a string of sunny days without any storms, I suspected that the A/C unit was the likely culprit. The A/C company reluctantly returned and realized that a hose had become plugged up, so the unit was discharging water. They fixed the hose and agreed to install a large metal pan below the unit (in the ceiling) to mitigate the issue, at no charge. But now our leak had become more consequential; wallboard would need to be replaced, and the repairs would include painting. We obtained an estimate of about $1,000 to cover the repairs. At the next monthly board meeting, I proposed that we should write to the A/C company and request that they cover the repair bill, since their "misdiagnosis" had resulted in the subsequent damage. The board agreed, though they were skeptical about whether we would be reimbursed. After a couple of months we did receive a check for the repairs, and an apology, though what was most important was the good will the exchange generated.

Other issues that arose over the course of my tenure included parking lot mishaps, such as the patron who drove over one of the parking berms. A snowplow driver had unwittingly dislodged the concrete barrier, and when the patron put her car in reverse, the berm became stuck under the car. One of the local mechanics came and helped dislodge it, with no apparent consequences. We did ask the patron to monitor her car for problems, and we offered to pay for any repairs, but we never heard anything further. In another instance, one of our high school workers ran into the book drop with her car, leaving a huge dent in both. Her insurance covered her car, and a local auto-repair shop volunteered to bang the dent out of the book drop. The book drop at one of our branch libraries had a different challenge. In the summertime, black snakes liked to nest in the bottom of the container. One of the branch workers took care of that problem. She relocated the nest to her barn, where the snakes were a natural pest control for the mice there; this solution reminded us that some facility challenges are more easily resolved than others.

Physical Security

In the library environment, there are various types of security issues to address. The issues to consider in emergency situations are primarily about structural damage and physical safety. After catastrophic events, especially natural disasters, structural damage may occur, even though it may not be obvious at first. Figure 5.1 lists the FEMA disaster declarations that were related to building damage, from 1953 through March 2019 (from their *Post-Disaster Building Safety Evaluation Guidance* manual). Most of these declarations were due to flooding and severe storms.

Even if there is no obvious loss of structural integrity, there may be other issues to contend with, such as nonfunctioning sewer systems, environmental hazards, or nonfunctioning utilities. Often a building inspection will be required before the facility can be entered, and certainly before the facility can return to normal functioning. During a declared disaster, qualified emergency response personnel will complete these assessments.

As a result of preliminary inspections, the building will be given a designation of either red (do not enter; unsafe to occupy, but not a demolition order); yellow (restricted use, with description of damages and corresponding cautionary measures), or green (inspected; lawful occupancy allowed). These designations will be posted on the building with a card of the corresponding color, making it easy to

FIGURE 5.1
FEMA building damage disaster declarations

Incident Type	Distinct Occurrences	Percentage of Total Declarations*
Flood	568	40.46%
Severe Storm(s)	378	26.92%
Tornado	143	10.19%
Hurricane	140	9.97%
Typhoon	41	2.92%
Fire	36	2.56%
Earthquake	20	1.42%
Freezing	14	1.00%
Coastal Storm	11	.78%
Severe Ice Storm	10	.71%
Snow	7	.50%
Volcano	4	.28%
Mud/Landslide	2	.14%
Dam/Levee Break	1	.07%
Human Cause	1	.07%
Terrorist	1	.07%

* Percentages above do not add up to 100% because disaster declaration data that do not result in building damage have not been included in the table.

determine which buildings and areas are safe, and which are not. The Chugiak-Eagle River Library field report in chapter 4 describes how the cards work in action.

Building safety evaluations are somewhat uniform, and for the most part, they do not change based on the type of emergency incident. These evaluations are a key activity, but they are just one of several things going on in a disaster situation. According to FEMA, these are the primary activities to expect after a disaster, listed in the order of their likely occurrence.

1. Incident occurs.
2. Initial information on the severity and location of damage is gathered.
3. First responders (i.e., fire and police personnel) make initial building assessments, restrict areas with hazardous conditions (e.g., downed power lines), and take injured people to appropriate medical care.
4. Local authorities and/or building officials conduct a windshield survey to assess the severity and spread of damage.
5. Search-and-rescue personnel locate and extricate people as needed.
6. If needed, the remains of deceased are recovered.
7. Utility personnel investigate and take care of gas leaks, downed power lines, and other hazards.
8. Post-disaster building safety evaluations are completed by trained personnel.
9. Limited reviews of nonstructural hazards and scans of environmental hazards are performed by building safety evaluators.
10. Environmental hazards are reviewed by personnel from agencies such as the local health department.
11. The building safety evaluation process continues, with cordons or barricades as needed.

This stepped process has worked well in the past, but it requires planning, training, and clearly defined roles and expectations; there are some financial assistance programs that can help with building safety evaluations after a disaster (www.fema.gov/assistance/public).

Ensuring physical safety for library workers and library users is essential and ongoing. Regular practices such as safety training, routine drills, and random checks for things such as problematic extension cords or other hazards can help to foster a safety mindset in the organization. You should consider collecting data from library users as well; for example, ask an amenable patron if they are willing to provide guidance on any flaws, and ways to improve accessibility, or to point out issues that may not have been considered. If needed, borrow a wheelchair, and at a regular staff meeting simulate a drill that requires evacuating the building when there is no electricity. For example, are there ramps or adequate curb breaks on the sidewalks that lead to the specified gathering place in case of evacuation?

For some security concerns, the obvious recourse is to use outside experts in the form of emergency responders, such as when a patron exhibits threatening behavior. One such case occurred while the author worked as a public library director, as described in "The Thursday Evening Shift" below.

---------- **The Thursday Evening Shift** ----------

IN THIS INSTANCE, a patron made inappropriate comments to one of the high school workers (who was a minor) and opened his coat to reveal that he was not wearing pants. This happened during the 5:00-9:00 p.m. shift, on a Thursday evening, so the staff wrote up an incident report, which I found on my desk the following morning. The report also stated that this man had been in the library twice before on Thursday evenings, had given off a "creepy vibe," and he "liked to hang around in the stacks." It happened that the staff assigned for the Thursday evening shift were two women: the high school worker and a full-time staff member who was in her late 20s.

After confirming the report with the full-time staff member who had been on duty, we looked at the security camera footage from the night before and found an image of the offender. I walked down to the police department and explained the situation. They advised us to call them immediately if he showed up again. I also asked if they would provide training so that workers could be prepared for these types of situations. That afternoon, the mother of the high school worker stopped by to express concern for her daughter's safety at the library. I was able to tell her that we had already contacted the police, and that for the next shifts when her daughter was working, we would have extra staff, and that I would also remain in the library on Thursday evenings. Two weeks later, the perpetrator showed up. We called the police, and they arrived quickly and quietly, and found the man in the stacks. They escorted him to a little-used exit, and advised him not to return. In the subsequent weeks, we learned that the man had been visiting libraries across the region, different libraries on different nights, and had caused concern everywhere he went. After his encounter with the police, he stopped visiting the libraries in our region.

The Haskell Free Library & Opera House has a unique set of considerations when it comes to maintaining physical security. The century-old library and opera house is in a building that was deliberately situated to straddle the U.S. and Canadian border, as a symbol and demonstration of friendship and cooperation. Although the two libraries are physically situated in two different countries and towns (Derby Line, Vermont, and Stanstead, Quebec), they share one building. A line made of electrical tape demarcates the international boundary, with 60 percent of the building and books in Canada. If there is a program or performance, the upstairs audience is in the United States, and the performers are in Quebec. Thus, in this town that is split down the middle, residents of both countries can interact without having to go through a border crossing. There is only one entrance to the building, through the U.S. side, and it is monitored twenty-four hours a day by the U.S. Department of Homeland Security. There are clear directions on where to park, and how to enter and exit the building for patrons from the Canadian side. No exchange of goods is allowed; that must take place under the jurisdiction of the Customs office.

This unique situation doesn't come without challenges. In 2019, there was a cross-border plot to smuggle dozens of firearms from Vermont into Quebec. The police were alerted when the library director, Nancy Rumery, noticed some irregularities. During the winter season when the rest of the community was wearing Canadian winter boots and heavy parkas, she reported that a "guy came in and he looked like he had stepped right out of GQ . . . he's in this beautifully tailored outfit and expensive leather boots" (Kassam quoting Rumery, 2018). Her instincts were right, as it turned out: the Canadian citizen in the fancy boots had coordinated with a pair of U.S. citizens to use the library bathroom as a drop-off point to smuggle backpacks filled with handguns. The attentive director thwarted the plan.

There are benefits to this type of boundary-spanning as well. In recent years, before COVID-19 necessitated closing the facility, the library was a hub for divided families, such as the Syrian family living in Toronto who were able to visit with their U.S. relatives at the library. During the COVID-19 pandemic the library has been closed, and because of its unique physical location, it will remain closed until the international border opens for nonessential travel. The library does offer other ways for patrons to use its resources during the shutdown, such as e-books, online access to databases, and contactless delivery (Haskell Free Library & Opera House 2021).

The library's efforts to serve communities on both sides of town, and in both countries, is clearly evident. For example, the website's resources list for COVID-19 information states that the library is dedicated to providing reliable information for the public in both the United States and Canada. The site then provides links to the U.S. Centers for Disease Control and Prevention, the World Health Organization, the Vermont Department of Health, and to Quebec government websites (Haskell Free Library & Opera House 2021).

Every library has unique risks and benefits created by its structure, its layout, and its location. A library building that straddles an international border may be an exceptional case, but no matter what the location or circumstance, all libraries can benefit from regular, routine inspection and maintenance, and vigilance. Tools like checklists, conferring with community experts, and regular drills can all make the tasks straightforward and routinized, and thus easier on everyone in the short and long term.

REFERENCES

Boehm, Jessica. 2017. "Phoenix Fires Employees over Burton Barr Library Flooding." *The Republic*, October 27. AZ Central, www.azcentral.com/story/news/local/phoenix/2017/10/27/phoenix-fires-demotes-suspends-employees-over-burton-barr-library-flooding-disaster/807291001/.

Federal Emergency Management Agency. 2019. *Post-Disaster Building Safety Evaluation Guidance*. FEMA P-255. www.fema.gov/sites/default/files/2020-07/fema_p-2055_post-disaster_buildingsafety_evaluation_2019.pdf.

Haskell Free Library & Opera House. 2021. "Visiting Information." https://haskellopera.com/about-us/.

Kassam, Ashifa. 2018. "Gun-Smuggling Case Puts Spotlight on Library Straddling U.S.-Canada Border." *The Guardian*, January 31. www.theguardian.com/world/2018/jan/31/canada-border-library-gun-smuggling-case.

Miller, Annetta. 2005. "Nigerian Proverb." In *African Wisdom for Life*. Nairobi, Kenya: Paulines Publications Africa.

Quinlan, Hannah. 2021. "Mediterranean Recluse Spiders Identified in Campus Buildings." *The University Record*. University of Michigan. https://record.umich.edu/artBcles/mediterranean-recluse-spiders-identified-in-campus-buildings/.

CHAPTER 6

Archives and Special Collections

DISASTER MANAGEMENT FOR SPECIAL COLLECTIONS CAN PRESENT ADDITIONAL complications over those of general collections. In this chapter, we will outline how to manage special collections throughout the disaster management cycle, and point to more specialized resources for format-specific guidance on disaster recovery.

Analog Collections

Archival and special collections require more attention in a disaster plan than other library materials because there is a heightened focus on damage prevention rather than on recovery actions. Analog materials—a term we use to refer to physical archival items such as books, manuscripts, documents, photographs, maps, and artifacts—are preserved because of their historical or evidential value, and their age makes them especially fragile. Moreover, their uniqueness makes them impossible or extremely challenging to replace, so the attitude toward disaster management in archives must therefore be one of proaction and not reaction. Many archives belong to larger institutions that often have an overarching disaster plan, but there may be little consideration of the archive specifically, so it helps to create a document for the archive that can be nested within the institution's policy.

This section will cover policies and organizational systems that can be adopted to better protect the materials in a special collection should a disaster occur; the information to include in a disaster plan for such collections; and restoration and conservation resources in the event that items need to be repaired.

While many severe weather events can be predicted, other disasters such as earthquakes, burst pipes, and fires can occur with no notice; and in any case, the time immediately before a disaster strikes is not the ideal time to begin rearranging materials. However, there are several steps that can be taken at any time to better prepare an archive for a disaster situation; many of these involve the organization of the collections. Of course, not every archive can implement every suggestion, due to time or storage constraints, but this can be mitigated by determining which disasters are more probable in a given region and then identifying the suggestions below that would be the most effective.

Rare book and manuscript collections are stored on shelving units to maximize vertical space and maintain visibility and access. Perhaps most important, both for damage mitigation and general safety, is to ensure that the shelving units are fastened to a wall, or else the floor, and thus will not topple over. High shelves should be equipped with a railing or other means of securing books or boxes during an earthquake, and it is convenient to reserve the upper shelves for the storage of lesser-used items. Keeping the bottom shelves empty of materials gives valuable inches of clearance in the event of a flood and is a low-maintenance strategy that can buy additional time to evacuate items before they are destroyed by water. If there is not sufficient storage space to leave ground-level shelves empty, you should prioritize which items are kept there; consider items that would have the least impact on the overall collection if they were destroyed, or would be the least difficult to replace.

It is also important to identify and clearly mark the most valuable items in the archive, whether that value be in research, money, or another factor. Such a mark should be externally visible (perhaps a colored sticker on the spine), have its meaning understood by all staff, and be explained in a master list that is easily accessible in the event of a disaster; if it is necessary and possible to evacuate materials, the most valuable items should be removed first. First responders or officials may be the only people authorized to enter the space immediately after a disaster, so having a map of where high-value items and collections are located and what they look like may allow non-staff to help. Being able to provide blueprints and engineering diagrams for the archive may also be important if a leaking pipe needs to be shut off or the building needs additional support after an earthquake; this includes valve, HVAC, plumbing, and plumbing riser plans. Newer buildings may also have "building information models," which are virtual, three-dimensional representations of the building and consolidate the plans listed above into one resource. For archives located within a larger library or on an institutional campus, this documentation is probably located in a maintenance office that may not actually be in the same building. In an emergency, it is best to have all potentially necessary technical plans easily accessible and to know what they are.

As was noted for libraries in chapter 2, establishing and maintaining relationships with local officials and first responders as an ongoing habit can help them respond more efficiently and effectively to emergency situations at the archives. Inviting responders to regularly tour the space, educating them about what materials are kept there, and consulting with them before purchasing safety equipment (e.g., fire suppression and security systems) can help them streamline and prioritize their efforts. Developing a familiarity with the building, collections, and staff over time will lead to a much greater and more comprehensive understanding of the archives than relying on brief moments during a disaster.

When a pipe bursts, a fire starts, or some other trigger happens, every second counts; any time saved by preparing beforehand will directly result in fewer damaged or destroyed materials. But even when every suggestion above is implemented and maintained, destruction cannot be prevented, it can only be mitigated and delayed. During a disaster, the following information must be retrievable at a moment's notice by any staff member, with or without electricity or internet connectivity. The master list of markings, schematic diagrams of the space, and maps of collections gathered according to the above guidance should be kept, together, digitally in a cloud environment and on individual computers and physically in offices, staff rooms, and perhaps even at home. Additionally, a predetermined information dissemination schedule, or phone tree, is an efficient means of communicating with staff while not burdening a single person with the need to contact everyone at the organization during a disaster. Contact information should be verified at regular intervals and should also include individuals' relevant strengths, such as their familiarity with public speaking, their ability to liaise with officials outside of the institution, and even their organizational and record-keeping skills.

For weather disasters, the hours and days leading up to and immediately following a severe storm are typically characterized by a flurry of activity as residents and businesses alike try to stock up on emergency necessities. If there is space at the library, consider keeping a "stockpile" of items that may be needed during or after a disaster but which may be in high demand and difficult to purchase in the moment. Depending on the disasters relevant to the region, this list should look different, but below are some basic items:

- Shop vacuumer
- Rags, towels, and so on
- Tarps
- Fans
- Space heater
- Generator
- Flashlights
- Batteries
- Radio
- Shovel
- Drinking water
- Nonperishable food
- Blankets
- Hand warmers
- Sandbags

It may not be practical to purchase items in advance and store them until they are needed. However, it may still be helpful to keep a list of things that might be useful, along with information on how to purchase them (store location, online order form, etc.), so that when they are needed, they can be acquired efficiently.

In the unfortunate event that collections are damaged, there are many conservation resources available. The Northeast Document Conservation Center (NEDCC) in Massachusetts offers conservation services for paper-based archival materials and preservation services for digital and audio materials in the greater New England area and throughout the United States. The NEDCC also creates educational content to enable archivists and special collections librarians to develop an understanding of conservation work and what work they can perform on their own.

The American Institute for Conservation (AIC) and the Foundation for Advancement in Conservation (FAIC), both headquartered in Washington, DC, work together to promote the preservation and conservation of cultural heritage resources on a nationwide and international scale. The AIC fosters research and education in the field by publishing peer-reviewed articles and books, and also supports a searchable network of conservation professionals and services in the United States and other countries. The National Heritage Responders, a team initiated by the FAIC after the devastation of Hurricanes Katrina and Rita in Louisiana, is a group of volunteer conservators, archivists, and other cultural heritage professionals who offer emergency support via e-mail and telephone hotline to institutions. In extreme emergencies, the group is deployed to the site of a major disaster for hands-on assistance.

Digital Collections

As with analog materials, born-digital and digitized archival materials come in a variety of file formats and accordingly must be treated with care. Throughout the remainder of this chapter, special collections materials created in a digital environment will be referred to as *born-digital collections or materials*, and special collections converted to a digital format from an analog format will be referred to as *digitized collections or materials*. There is overlap in how these materials are treated, but the distinction between them is sometimes necessary. *Digital collections or materials* will be used as an umbrella term to refer to both types of special collections.

Contrary to popular belief, digital collections can be more fragile than their analog counterparts. Digital fragility is not a new concept, but it is increasingly relevant for digital archives as file formats evolve and become obsolete. Access and usability are key considerations when assessing risk and creating disaster recovery protocols for digital archives. Materials in obsolete proprietary formats are especially vulnerable, and information professionals should advocate to reformat them when possible. If such materials are corrupted or damaged during a disaster, it may be difficult to find a subject expert to work with them, depending on the age or obsolescence of the format. The mundane details of converting file formats for collections are thus necessary to prevent losing the records contained within them. Data loss through format degradation is a disaster in itself.

Reformatting, especially in old or rare formats, can be very costly in the long term. If you are having trouble making the case to your library director, board, or other authority to get funds for reformatting, research the average life spans of the formats you are working with as a benchmark of how long the information stored on these formats will be stable. There are a number of grants available for digitizing or reformatting historically significant media.

Given the importance of ensuring the authenticity of archival materials, the chain of custody must be ensured throughout the disaster recovery process. Tracking digital collections, as with analog materials, is thus essential. Good and clear description, along with record-keeping about how digital collections are handled, is useful for disaster management. Make sure your staff understand how to document any changes they make to digital collections according to the policies and procedures of your institution.

DISTRIBUTED STORAGE

It is now common practice for special collections to keep multiple copies of their digital collections stored in at least two different locations. This risk management strategy is meant to protect against material loss if one data center is compromised during a regional disaster. Many institutions have joined digital preservation consortia to share the responsibilities of stewarding their digital collections—including risk management. Consortia may be able to negotiate more favorable service contracts with vendors, and the members of a consortium can draw upon each other's expertise to strengthen their digital preservation practices.

Academic Preservation Trust

AN INTERVIEW WITH BRADLEY DAIGLE AND FLAVIA RUFFNER
BY MICHELLE RUNYON

THE ACADEMIC PRESERVATION Trust, colloquially known as APTrust, is a digital preservation consortium in which the members jointly store digital assets. It is run in conjunction with the University of Virginia's libraries. The consortium was initially geared toward academic libraries, though increasingly public libraries and other cultural heritage institutions are joining it. Bradley Daigle, the executive director of APTrust, has held various positions with the University of Virginia and APTrust. Flavia Ruffner is APTrust's development and security lead engineer, and previously worked for Information Technology Services at the University of Virginia. Michelle Runyon, a coauthor of this chapter, is a member of the APTrust Advisory Committee and the digital archivist at the College of William & Mary.

Transparency is a core value for APTrust. The consortium provides access to robust documentation for members and the public alike. Its policies and governing principles are freely available online. APTrust's Trusted Digital Repository certification process was the immediate impetus for creating its initial disaster recovery plan. The initial draft of this plan includes a list of potential risks to the consortium members' digital collections, along with proposed mitigation strategies. The consortium's Communications and Policy Group collaborated with the Trusted Digital Repository Working Group to create the disaster recovery plan. Brad Daigle was involved in the creation of the first draft of the plan. Daigle, a member of the Digital Preservation Coalition's governance management group, has experience in risk mitigation. The DPC has a robust disaster plan, which it uses for internal purposes. From his experience with the DPC, Daigle would like to see, in the final version of APTrust's own disaster recovery plan, the risks listed and ranked by how likely they are to occur, what organizational area(s) they pertain to, and what mitigation strategies might prevent them from occurring.

Daigle became especially concerned about disaster planning after attending a LOCKSS (Lots of Copies Keep Stuff Safe) workshop called "Risks to Digital Information" at the International Conference on Massive Storage Systems and Technology. Many of the topics that LOCKSS staff members discussed in this workshop were addressed, along with risk mitigation strategies, in the first draft of APTrust's disaster recovery plan. Once the final version of the disaster plan is completed, there will be a publicly accessible narrative outline of the plan alongside a more detailed internal document.

However, the transparency of APTrust's disaster recovery plan is also its catch-22. If transparent and publicly accessible, the plan will be more useful to more institutions—but it will also be open to bad agents like hackers who could compromise our digital assets. This balance, difficult to strike, was the subject of many internal discussions about whether or not to make any part of the policy public. To Daigle's knowledge, there are no other consortia of comparable size that make even part of their disaster plan public. Daigle, Ruffner, and myself all hope that transparency about the APTrust disaster planning process will inspire the digital preservation community to more openly discuss how digital archival assets are protected by various services. The lack of transparency about digital preservation failures and risk management is already a concern (Dearborn and Meister 2017). Ruffner notes that with the increasing use of cloud storage, many preservationists would probably appreciate more information about how the assets stored in cloud systems are stewarded and how risks are mitigated. An additional hope for the APTrust community is that transparency about our disaster planning will, internally, build more support for the consortium's mission—and externally, attract more institutions to join the consortium. Hopefully, this will enable members to effectively measure risk for their assets and understand when to take individual actions that are not covered by the APTrust consortial agreement.

Flavia Ruffner and I are currently revising the disaster recovery plan. Ruffner is in charge of security for APTrust—another benefit of having her involved in the disaster planning process. At the time of this writing, Ruffner and I have reviewed the first draft of the disaster recovery plan and are trying to appropriately scope out what topics should be covered by the plan in its final form, as well as what may be best addressed in other APTrust documentation. In particular, Ruffner and I are reviewing what library- or archives-specific standards to incorporate into our next draft of the disaster recovery plan.

Disaster management for a digital preservation consortium requires cohesive organizational structure and a variety of interdisciplinary skills. The need for stable communication and clear planning cannot be overstated. One strength of APTrust is its regular two- to three-year schedule for reviewing and modifying documentation, which allows members to give input and shape APTrust to be in line with industry best practices. From the beginning, our team has been intentional about having a manageable, regularly maintained disaster plan. Beyond mere documents and policies, Daigle and Ruffner both stress that it is vital to have leadership that supports and prioritizes disaster planning. If management lacks a clear vision of what needs to be accomplished, risk management can easily fall to the wayside.

Given the interdisciplinary nature of disaster management, especially for digital preservation, Daigle and Ruffner both shared what they wished others with different expertise understood about their role in stewarding digital assets for cultural heritage institutions. Daigle wants IT professionals to understand that these collections aren't monoliths. Each digital collection is complex and has its own intricacies. A one-size-fits-all approach will not work for the diversity of archival digital objects that an organization like APTrust stewards. Ruffner says that librarians need to create systems that fit their requirements and that IT should support them. Most crucially, effective systems must be built with *users* in mind. This requires IT professionals to review, often at a granular level, how individuals in an organization accomplish tasks and how their workflows come to be. Ruffner notes that designing an IT system necessitates discovering what you don't know. APTrust is familiar with running into the blind spots of an IT system.

While APTrust has not experienced any major disasters, there have been minor incidents and near-incidents which required technical and organizational finesse to navigate effectively. One time, a database structural error caused a member institution's upload of a collection saved as null files. APTrust's lead developer, Andrew Diamond, quickly resolved the error, and the member institution re-uploaded their collection files from a backup without issue. Undergoing the Trusted Digital Repository self-audit process also helped APTrust take measures to reduce human error or malfeasance when managing collection files—a good example of how external review strengthens disaster management.

Disaster management for born-digital cultural heritage organizations is still an emerging topic in digital preservation. We hope that this early glimpse into APTrust's disaster planning will encourage more conversation about how to better safeguard our digital legacy.

Service disruption is also an important consideration in storing digital collections. It is important for institutions to establish an exit strategy to pull their collections out of storage if the vendor they work with goes out of business or radically alters its service in a way that is no longer favorable to the institution.

LEVELS OF ACCESS

Maintaining the ability to mediate access to special collections materials during a disaster is crucial. Many special collections have sensitive materials, and it would be disastrous if they were exposed during a data breach. This is why most special collections have different levels of access to digital archives. A public-facing site will typically have access copies, while a dark archive will have originals or master files. With any dark archive, it is important to limit who can and cannot access it. There should also be robust measures for users to authenticate their identities, through two-factor authentication or other means. Institutions should limit the number of users who can access their dark archive and what permissions each user has to edit or manipulate collection content. Collections materials with sensitive information, including personally identifiable information, should be given special attention, and will require additional safeguards so they are not accidentally exposed to a patron or a bad agent like a hacker. This could include encrypting the data in question or requiring dual-factor authentication to access it.

Various types of sensitive information can be found in digital collections, including FERPA- or HIPAA-protected information. To maintain the confidentiality of those who are discussed in these records, library staff should review incoming library materials for sensitive information with tools like the bulk extractor from Bitcurator. If there is sensitive content in the collection materials, library staff will probably need to isolate it from the collections that don't have sensitive information so they can apply greater protections to the sensitive content. Library staff should regularly review the relevant legal requirements for how to treat various types of sensitive information.

In addition to collection materials, it is also important to safeguard donors' and users' information. Donor agreements, user records, and other similar materials likely contain sensitive information that should be treated securely.

Recovery for Rare Materials

There are a number of conservators who specialize in working with materials in a variety of formats. While conservators and consultants' lists change over time, we have included resources where you and your library staff can find potential conservation assistance. If your institution undergoes a risk assessment, this can be a good time to identify the specialized skills needed to salvage and recover your holdings. Documenting your at-risk and fragile special collections will make setting priorities for conservation interventions easier in the event of an emergency. It is easiest to document what materials may require preservation interventions if the staff are doing stacks maintenance regularly or otherwise reviewing their collections.

REFERENCE

Dearborn, Carly, and Sam Meister. 2017. "Failure as Process: Interrogating Disaster, Loss, and Recovery in Digital Preservation." *Alexandria: The Journal of National and International Library and Information Issues* 27, no. 2: 83–93.

CHAPTER 7

Looking Ahead
FUTURE OPPORTUNITIES

> We need joy as we need air. We need love as we need water.
> We need each other as we need the earth we share.
> —*Maya Angelou*

LIBRARIES HAVE BEEN DESCRIBED IN MANY WAYS OVER THE YEARS, FROM REPOSI-tories to incubators, to anchor organizations that are open to all. Given their embeddedness throughout communities and institutions, it is likely they will remain vital partners in our collective struggle for a more just society. At their core, libraries are about offering support, whether that comes in the form of information resources, materials, or a safe place. Social support has been shown to play a role in maintaining physical and psychological well-being and can increase resiliency towards stress (Ozbay et al. 2007). Thus, in challenging times, libraries are more important than ever.

The previous chapters have provided inspiring examples of ways libraries have aided their communities, and how communities in turn have fortified their libraries during adverse times. Because disasters are on the rise, there is increasing involvement of all types of libraries in community disaster management activities. This involvement can be as simple as practicing preparedness activities with staff, providing tools and program activities for library users, or providing a forum for training for local first responders on emergency apps.

As an information interlocutor for the community, the library already plays the essential role of ensuring that users have access to timely and accurate information, no matter the topic. In addition to authoritative information distribution, libraries can provide other tangible resources, such as updated flood zone maps, brochures on flood insurance, preparedness infographics, posters with information, and easy links on the library's website to preparedness tools. In this way, we can also help guard against the spread of misinformation which can so often occur during emergency situations.

As we embrace our role as information providers during emergency situations, a primary consideration is how we can ensure that information is accessible to all of our community members. In the following text box, Emily Vardell discusses literacy concerns with regard to disaster preparedness and response.

Literacy Concerns in Disaster Preparedness and Response

EMILY VARDELL

AS LIBRARIANS, WE focus on providing quality information to educate the public. This also applies to the roles librarians can fill in disaster preparedness and emergency response. However, a key piece of the puzzle that must not be overlooked is the role that literacy concerns play when talking about fostering a better-informed community.

Most of the online resources that have been created for the provision of disaster information are in English (with the occasional Spanish-language resource) and are often written at a higher reading level. While many of these are created for disaster response professionals (e.g., public health officials, firefighters, FEMA employees, etc.), many of them are also touted as resources for the general public. How truly accessible are these resources if they are only available in limited languages and are written at a higher reading level than the average individual can readily comprehend?

This issue most certainly came into the spotlight during the COVID-19 pandemic, when populations that have been shown to have lower literacy levels and higher levels of health disparities (e.g., minority populations, lower-income populations, etc.) were also the populations contracting and dying from COVID-19 at higher rates in the United States (Rossen et al. 2020). While there were many factors at play, one that most certainly should not be ignored is that of literacy.

When materials are created to help inform the public during a disaster, it is imperative that these literacy concerns are taken into consideration. This is one area in which infographics and other visual means are key. As we live through the COVID-19 pandemic at the time of this writing, it is quite common to see a sign depicting a person wearing a mask on the door of a place of business to indicate that the business requires individuals to wear a mask before entering, rather than just having the warning written out in English. This is a step in the right direction to ensure that individuals understand the necessary precautions with which to prepare and respond to disaster situations in their areas.

It is also a smart strategy to use readability checkers to review any materials that are created for the general public. There are several of these checkers freely available online for use, and even Microsoft Word has built-in features that individuals can use to assess materials (to access this, go to the File menu, then Options, then the Proofing tab where a "Show readability statistics" option is available). Some of these readability checkers may offer suggestions for how to lower the necessary reading level required to understand a document, but not all do. As a general rule of thumb, shorter words tend to be easier to comprehend for those with a lower reading ability, and tables with short phrases can be an effective way to convey a larger amount of information. If possible, it is always best practice to have individuals from the community you serve provide feedback on any materials you may plan to develop, since they can provide guidance on culturally appropriate terminology and recommendations.

Another best practice is to undertake community assessment projects in order to identify the needs in your area. Naturally this includes evaluating the most likely disasters to prepare for, but it also includes identifying the populations in your area. It is wise to not only collect information about the languages spoken and read in your community, but also information about whether populations might represent refugee, indigenous, or other special groups that may have unique information needs. As we know, words carry different meanings in different contexts and cultures. One version of a Spanish-language pamphlet may not be relevant to all Latinos/Latinas in your community, for example. This is where building partnerships with community organizations can be especially helpful and impactful. Churches, schools, and community organizations may be able to help librarians identify individuals within the different communities who can assist in creating culturally and linguistically appropriate materials for the people in your community.

As a medical librarian in southern Florida, I was part of a community health outreach project in which medical librarians would attend medical student-led community health fairs where individuals from the community could come for health assessments. Medical librarians would be on hand to provide health information about relevant conditions and helpful resources. We secured grant funding to translate some of our informational materials into Haitian Creole to help serve the Haitian population in southern Florida. It was only after we started distributing these materials at the fairs that we learned that many Haitian individuals (in particular older adults) had actually learned to read French in school rather than Haitian, and so our well-intentioned Haitian Creole materials were not useful to them. This is a good example of when it is helpful to get feedback from your community so that you can be culturally responsive. (In the end, we used additional grant funds to also translate the materials into French.)

If librarians are not reaching out to everyone in their communities, then they could be exacerbating issues of inequality and injustice with regard to who is able to appropriately prepare for disasters and who is able to get the help they need after a disaster occurs. It is imperative that librarians keep in mind whom they are serving when developing disaster information resources and outreach efforts.

REFERENCE

Rossen, L. M., A. M. Branum, F. B. Ahmad, P. Sutton, and R. N. Anderson. 2020. "Excess Deaths Associated with COVID-19, by Age and Race and Ethnicity—United States, January 26–October 3, 2020." *Morbidity and Mortality Weekly Report* 69: 1522–27.

Whether located on a campus or in a rural crossroads, the library is a significant cornerstone of community function. This role becomes even more important during disaster events, when the library can be a vital partner for helping communities cope with crises. Because they are usually centrally located, with easy public access, libraries often become the hub for resource distribution beyond information and routine library lending. This might include items like canned goods, bleach, and bottled water during emergencies.

Library facilities are built for accommodating visitors, so they are logical facilities to serve as warming and cooling places for more vulnerable segments of the population. These activities have to be planned for, however, with a commitment to procuring the necessary support systems, such as staff buy-in, generators (in case of power outages), and emergency supplies. Another practical way that libraries can lend community support is for library workers to train as disaster response specialists, as discussed by Emily Vardell in the text box below.

Preparing Librarians to Serve as Trained Disaster Response Specialists

EMILY VARDELL

BECAUSE THEY ARE uniquely skilled as both knowledge managers and community liaisons, librarians are well positioned to help institutions and organizations prepare and respond to disasters. There has been a growing awareness of the importance of librarian involvement as disaster response specialists in a variety of settings, including academic health science libraries (Featherstone 2012), hospital libraries (Donahue and Featherstone 2013), and public libraries (Davis and Jankow 2019). What is less clear is how librarians are becoming trained to serve in such capacities, whether that occurs in library science graduate school coursework or through continuing education opportunities.

There are currently only a small handful of library and information science (LIS) programs that offer courses in disaster preparedness, including Emporia State University (in a course entitled "Disaster Preparedness and Emergency Response"), the University of North Texas (in a course entitled "Disaster/Emergency Management for Information Professionals"), the University of North Carolina at Chapel Hill (in a course entitled "Disaster Planning for Libraries"), and San Jose State University (in a course entitled "Crisis/Disaster Health Informatics").

The "Disaster Preparedness and Emergency Response" course offered at Emporia State University, for example, is an optional elective that counts towards both the Health Information Professionals Certificate and the Health Information Professionals Concentration. The course offers students the opportunity to explore in-depth what librarians can do to prepare and respond to disasters and emergency situations. Topics within the course syllabus include disaster information resources, librarian roles, specific disaster types (e.g., pandemics, tornadoes, fires, etc.), literacy concerns, and librarian self-care in disasters. Students are asked to review the disaster plans they are able to locate from library websites as an environmental scan of available information resources. The main assignment for the course is a one-page service continuity plan that students develop either for a library where they are currently employed or for another library of their choosing.

One of the more unique aspects of the course is that as the instructor, I invite practicing librarians and other information professionals to speak about their own work experiences relating to disasters that have occurred in their libraries (including tornadoes, fire, earthquakes, floods, hurricanes, and violence). As one student remarked in the end-of-semester course evaluations, "so much learning takes place beyond the textbook, and having the opportunity to hear from those who have experienced emergencies and disasters allowed us to build on their combined knowledge."

Disaster preparedness content is not a required element for any ALA-accreditation measurements. However, to address this important aspect of preparing future librarians, general LIS courses (including core courses) may include elements of disaster preparedness within the curriculum. For example, management courses may discuss best practices for emergency response as well as how to develop a disaster plan. This content could also be embedded in consumer health, social justice, and community outreach courses.

The need to learn about disaster preparedness and response does not end once the master of library science degree is achieved. Many librarians in the field may find that they need to acquire more skills and knowledge in this area when they are tasked with writing their library's disaster plan or when, in the event, they must respond to a disaster or emergency in their library. Several professional organizations and outlets (including the American Library Association, the Medical Library Association, the Public Library Association, state library associations, and WebJunction) have responded to this need and have offered continuing education (CE) or webinars on these topics.

The National Library of Medicine and the Medical Library Association (MLA) partnered to create the Disaster Information Specialization (www.mlanet.org/education/dis/) for practicing information professionals. This specialist program/specialization, now maintained by the MLA and the University of Virginia, is comprised of free online training courses developed by the NLM and FEMA to train librarians and other "information responders" in accessing and using disaster health information. The MLA page clearly states that the specialization is designed not only for librarians, library staff, and information professionals, but also for disaster workforce members, including health care providers, allied health professionals, public health workers, first responders, and more. Those interested in obtaining the specialization can do so at the Basic Level (15 CE credit hours) or the Advanced Level (27 credit hours). The MLA specialization is valid for three years and requires an application fee.

Librarians can fill a wide variety of roles in disaster preparedness and emergency response—from preserving collections, to ensuring the continuity of library operations, to serving as embedded disaster information specialists within their communities. Library science programs and professional associations can and should continue to explore methods for helping librarians to develop these skills and prepare to serve as disaster response specialists.

REFERENCES

Davis, Adam S., and Chris Jankow. 2019. "On Why Library Workers Are Well-Suited to Serve during Disasters." *Collaborative Librarianship* 11, no. 1: 1-4.

Donahue, Amy E., and Robin M. Featherstone. 2013. "New Roles for Hospital Librarians: A Benchmarking Survey of Disaster Management Activities." *Journal of the Medical Library Association* 101, no. 4: 315-18.

Featherstone, Robin M. 2012. "The Disaster Information Specialist: An Emerging Role for Health Librarians. *Journal of Library Administration* 52, no. 8: 731-53.

Engagement with other library workers beyond our immediate local and state boundaries is another way to learn about and become involved in disaster management activities. The next text box, "Paying It Forward," describes the hopefulness engendered by providing support for a library that is recovering from a disaster.

LOOKING AHEAD | 127

Paying It Forward

AS DESCRIBED IN chapter 2 (in the section titled "Mitigation, Too?"), the author was working as a public library director during a catastrophic flood event in June 2006. Less than a year *before* that event occurred, the country was rocked by extensive damage from Hurricane Katrina in late August, particularly in Louisiana and Mississippi. Reports of devastated communities and libraries left many of us contemplating ways we could lend support to our beleaguered colleagues. One story in particular resonated. The public library in Pass Christian, Mississippi (a town similar in size to our library's own community) had just finished major renovations in August 2005, at the start of the month in which Katrina hit. The library staff were very excited to share the new facility, which had even been placed on the Historical Society's annual tour. When the town was inundated by the epic hurricane, the new library building was totally demolished, with a loss of more than 35,000 items. After I shared this story at our regular Friends of the Library board meeting in September 2005, they decided to send a monetary donation to help with rebuilding.

The Pass Christian library was able to reopen in November 2005 in the town's War Memorial Park with the donation of two trailers from a local plant. They operated using trailers until June 2010 (on the library's 37th anniversary), when they became the first post-Katrina, newly built public library to open on Mississippi's Gulf Coast (Pham-Bui 2010).

On a side note, while Katrina was pounding the town, police officers and the police chief moved to take shelter in the new library building, which had been designed to withstand hurricane winds, and was located at one of the higher elevations in town. As the floodwater level rose above four feet, the police chief realized the police cars that were in the library's parking lot would float, and one of them might hit the building and crash through the library doors; he knew they all had to get out immediately. They tried to shoot out some windows, to no avail; they were reinforced glass. As a last resort, the police chief swam to the rear exit door and pushed it open. His colleagues were sure he would be swept away, but because the chief had toured the library facility repeatedly, he knew there were railings right by the rear door. He was able to grab on to a railing and remain safe. All the other officers were able to make it to the roof, where they rode out the storm (Savidge 2005).

Months later, in the midst of our own flood clean-up at the Sidney Library (in upstate New York), one of the Friends' board members recalled our contribution to Pass Christian and realized that when the check was sent to support the Gulf Coast community this was, in a sense, "paying it forward." She added, gratefully, that at least in Sidney there was still an intact library building that they could clean and salvage.

Final Thoughts

Though disaster preparedness requires an ongoing organizational commitment and may seem like a daunting endeavor, even a minimal disaster plan can save time and frustration, and result in stress reduction. You should start with making community connections; it is likely many of these are already in place and can be readily built upon. Proper caretaking of the collection is another easy step, such as performing regular maintenance activities, like weeding and identifying and securing valuable items. If the library is the repository for the town's local history or genealogy documents, make sure that these are not stored in areas that might be vulnerable to unexpected hazards, such as flooding or mildew. This will make salvage activities, if they're ever needed, much more streamlined and responsive. Encourage the staff to engage in continuing education opportunities, such as workshops, webinars, and conferences. Regular drills for library workers, and maintenance and inspection schedules for the physical facility, are other relatively straightforward ways to instigate a preparedness mindset on an organizational level.

Learn how *your* library can support *your* community. For instance, if there is an expectation in the town that the library will be the ad hoc food bank as needed during crises, investigate ahead of time what this might entail. Is there room for such an activity, are library workers on board, and who will be the community partners? Try to think outside the box, as we have seen time and again in the library sphere. For example, in hurricane-prone eastern North Carolina, a book drop served as a canned food repository. During the COVID-19 pandemic, the Jaffrey Public Library in New Hampshire geared up with the "Monadnock doll hospital" to help reduce fear of vaccines. Children could bring their dolls and stuffed animals to the library to be "vaccinated" (Hub 2021). Likewise, probably thousands of libraries have provided access to internet hubs during the COVID pandemic, even when they were physically closed.

Given that many of our disaster challenges can be tied to our changing climate, you should consider hosting discussions or programs on climate change and our national dependence on fossil fuels. This could be followed up with a program on resilient building practices. If there is an opportunity for construction or rebuilding, do so thoughtfully and intentionally with regard to renewable resources.

Finally, in a webinar on disaster preparedness, the author was asked some thought-provoking questions. One attendee asked how to get reluctant partners and staff on board for disaster planning. For instance, how do you convince the IT department and the finance folks that there is a need for preparedness against cyberattacks? Another questioner asked if staff safety training should be mandatory.

When it comes to working with other departments such as IT, I have found that it helps to supply facts and hard data that illustrate how important prevention and preparedness can be. For example, the ransomware attacks described in chapter 2 could be shared to demonstrate that while libraries may not be regular targets, they can be vulnerable, and attacks can be expensive.

In terms of engaging library workers, my advice would be to start by asking them how they would like to approach disaster preparedness, and what kind of training and tools they could use. Should the library offer programs, or just take advantage of National Preparedness month (September) to highlight the resources that are available? You should proactively provide opportunities for staff to offer input, including making time to address any reservations they might have. This could happen in a variety of ways, starting with one-on-one meetings to assess individual staff members' concerns and interests. A dedicated staff meeting or an in-service day could be used to conduct or update risk assessments or to build go-bags. Ask each team member to find a recent library disaster, or choose their favorite disaster game, and then allocate time to discuss these during regular meetings.

Hopefully you will never have to fully employ your disaster plan, but those folks who have helped their communities through disaster response and recovery all agree that having a plan and thinking ahead did help, and it did have a positive impact on overall morale and outcomes. An ounce of prevention may well be worth a pound of cure.

REFERENCES

Angelou, Maya. 2018. Twitter post. June 29. https://twitter.com/drmayaangelou/status/1012759173048696834?lang=en.

The Hub. 2021. "Monadnock Doll Hospital Returns to Jaffrey Library." *Sentinel Source.* www.sentinelsource.com/hub/news/community_news/monadnock-doll-hospital-returns-to-the-jaffrey-library/article_c92b5ab1-ed24-5e0f-a628-0ff77e95f5d0.html.

Ozbay, Fatih, Douglas C. Johnson, Eleni Dimoulas, C. A. Morgan III, Dennis Charney, and Steven Southwick. 2007. "Social Support and Resilience to Stress: From Neurobiology to Clinical Practice." *Psychiatry (Edgmont)* 4, no. 5: 35.

Pham-Bui, Trang. 2010. "First Shipment of Books Arrives at New Pass Christian Library." *WLOX News.* www.wlox.com/story/12309525/first-shipment-of-books-arrives-at-new-pass-christian-library/.

Savidge, Martin. 2005. "Shootout at Pass Christian." *The Daily Nightly,* MSNBC. https://web.archive.org/web/20141022165219/http:/dailynightly.msnbc.com/2005/11/shootout_at_pas.html.

APPENDIX
Model Memorandum of Understanding, National Library of Medicine

The following model Memorandum of Understanding has been endorsed by the NNLM Southeastern/Atlantic region of the National Library of Medicine.

Model Memorandum of Understanding for a Health Sciences, Hospital/System, or Medical Library for Emergency Preparedness Support

This Memorandum of Understanding (MOU) is a mutual aid agreement and a totally voluntary program between cooperating 'partner' libraries.

Purpose:

The purpose of the MOU is to establish a working relationship between hospital or health system 'partner' libraries as follows:

_____

and

_____

It provides an agreement to assist the partner library in one or more ways during a disaster which "exceeds the effective response capability of the impacted health care facility or facilities," or in the event of local power, electronic systems, or communications outages which impact upon the partner library's ability to provide needed and/or essential information for its users, clients and patrons. It outlines the ways personnel, services and communications can be conducted in time of emergencies. The cooperation of the "partner/buddy" libraries is considered a best practice, and for hospital libraries is recommended by JCAHO standard, IM.5.10 and EC.4.10.15.

Modifications/Severance

This MOU provides flexibility for changing the parameters of mutual aid or the ability to discontinue partnership at any time. It is for this reason this model recommends that a library have more than one partner library in the event of a disaster and that partner libraries have one library at a minimum that is geographically disparate and/or distinct from the partner.

Definition of a Disaster

A disaster is an occurrence such as a hurricane, tornado, storm, flood, high water, wind-driven water, tidal wave, earthquake, drought, blizzard, pestilence, famine, fire, explosion, building collapse, transportation wreck, terrorist event, bioterrorist event, pandemic, power failure, or other similar natural or man-made incident(s) that causes human suffering or creates human needs that require assistance of hospitals, healthcare personnel as well as the support of libraries in aid of hospitals, healthcare personnel, first responders, or public health personnel.

Other events covered by this agreement include power, telephone and electronic systems outages in the partner institution.

The following outlines the services, personnel, and support agreed upon by partner libraries during a disaster or other covered event as well as protocols and cost recovery.

Method of Cooperation

On a biannual basis the cooperating libraries will communicate to update each library about any mutual developments related to this MOU. Both libraries will review contact information and agreed-upon services and make modifications as needed in writing. In the event a particular need is previously unforeseen, partner libraries may amend this MOU and document changes on the MOU at the earliest possible convenience.

Responsibilities of the Library Partners

ACTIVATION/WARNING/COMMUNICATIONS

The following items should be completed as agreed to by the partner libraries and detailed below and/or with an attached Addenda (if more space is needed).

Determine how and when to request activation of support during a disaster or if there is a need to advise a partner there may be a need to activate, depending upon weather or other warning systems.

_____

_____

_____

_____

Who to contact: (include staff tree, names, titles and/or alternates)

_____

_____

_____

_____

How to contact: (include phone tree, cell phones, addresses, fax, email, and indication of home or office information)

_____

_____

_____

_____

In instances of telephone service interruption, establish preferred backup activation plan.

_____

_____

_____

_____

SERVICES OFFERED

(Check all that apply and specify definitions, parameters, or limits if any on attached page.)

- ☐ Interlibrary Loan (specify methods): _____
- ☐ Reference/Research
- ☐ Database or Literature Searches
- ☐ Consultation
- ☐ Bibliographies
- ☐ Retention/copies of the following:
  - ☐ OPAC (Online Public Access Catalog) Back-up
  - ☐ Insurance Policy
  - ☐ Emergency Plan and/or Disaster Recovery Plan
  - ☐ Other:

- ☐ Other: _____
- ☐ Other: _____
- ☐ Other: _____

COST RECOVERY

Partnering libraries agree that overhead costs such as personnel, telephones, Internet lines or other similar items will not be reimbursed. Direct out-of-pocket costs will be reimbursed by partner libraries. Costs under one hundred dollars ($100) can be made on behalf of the partner library. Costs over one hundred dollars ($100) should receive prior authorization first from the partner library before incurring the expense. Expenses that are considered direct out-of-pocket costs are courier, database searches (if vendor bills on a per search or time basis), document delivery, other:

_____

_____

_____

RECORD KEEPING:

A tracking system for costs incurred should be maintained by the cooperating library with date, cost, description of service, and receipt or invoice and name of requestor. As soon as is possible after the end of the precipitating disaster or other covered incident, the cooperating library will invoice the partner for these expenses. If the incident lasts longer than one week, the cooperating library may invoice periodically until the incident has ended.

Authorized Signatures

The undersigned are authorized to agree to this MOU on behalf of their Library. All rights reserved by each library providing copies and/or records. No part of any resource may be reproduced in any form without the prior written permission of the owner, except in instances where an archival or backup copy of an item is placed on another network for the purposes of this MOU. The undersigned libraries are not responsible for any errors, or any consequences caused as a result of the use, storage, or services provided via this MOU. This MOU is provided with the understanding that the libraries are not engaged in rendering any legal, accounting, or other professional services and shall not be held liable for any circumstances arising out of this voluntary program or the MOU. If legal advice or other expert assistance is required, the services of a competent professional should be sought.

Library Director Authorized Signature Partner Library 'A'

Print name: _____

Title: _____

Library: _____

Institution: _____

Address: _____

Date: _____

Library Director Authorized Signature Partner Library 'B'

Print name: _____

Title: _____

Library: _____

Institution: _____

Address: _____

Date: _____

Other Authorized Institutional Signature: Partner Library 'A'

Print name: _____

Title: _____

Library: _____

Institution: _____

Address: _____

Date: _____

Other Authorized Institutional Signature: Partner Library 'B'

Print name: _____

Title: _____

Library: _____

Institution: _____

Address: _____

Date: _____

Endorsed by the Health Sciences Library Association of New Jersey, October 19, 2005.

(Developed jointly by New Jersey Hospital Association, J. Harold Johnston Memorial Library, Michelle Volesko Brewer and Hackensack University Medical Center Medical Library, Barbara S. Reich. Edition 1, October 14, 2005.)

For suggestions or comments, please contact the authors at mmvbrewer@verizon.net or bsreich@gmail.com.

[CC BY-NC-SA]

This work is licensed under the Creative Commons Attribution-NonCommercial-ShareAlike 2.5 License. To view a copy of this license, visit http://creativecommons.org/licenses/by-nc-sa/2.5/ or send a letter to Creative Commons, 543 Howard Street, 5th Floor, San Francisco, California, 94105, USA.

MVB Model MOU rev6FINAL

INDEX

A

academic libraries
    with disaster plans in place, 15–16
    Emergency Preparedness Committee, 58–60
Academic Preservation Trust (APTrust), 116–118
Academy of Adventure Gaming Arts & Design, 34
access
    digital archives disaster recovery and, 115
    to digital archives, levels of, 118–119
accessibility, 106
active shooters, 50–51
After the Crisis: Using Storybooks to Help Children Cope (Grace & Shores), 46
aftershocks, 74
AIC (American Institute for Conservation), 9, 114
aid
    libraries and disaster planning, 8–10
    MOUs about, 9
air conditioning (A/C) unit, 95, 103–104
Alaska State Libraries, Archives and Museums, 102–103
alerts
    emergency alerts, 21
    for flooding, 91
    for tornadoes, 70
Allbaugh, Joe, 4
American Institute for Conservation (AIC), 9, 114
American Library Association (ALA)
    Adopt a Library Program after Hurricane Maria, 8
    COVID-19 Recovery site, 55
    Stafford Act amendment and, 7

American Red Cross
    civil unrest training, 54
    comfort, promoting, 43–44
    disaster preparedness games, resources for, 33
    disaster preparedness resources of, 20
    support of communities during disasters, 3
    training opportunities offered by, 28
analog collections, 111–114
Anchorage, Alaska, 75–79
Andrus, Miriam, 87–90
Angelou, Maya, 121
applications (apps), 21–22
APTrust (Academic Preservation Trust), 116–118
archives and special collections
    analog collections, 111–114
    digital collections, 114–119
    recovery of rare materials, 119
arson, 47, 52
assets, library, 31
ATI Restoration, 81
Atkins, Winston, 24–26
Australia, 47

B

backup, 32
Baker, Alia, xi
Baltimore County Public Library, 53
Barney, Gerald O., ix
Bartlett, John, 36
Battelle, 54
Bitcurator bulk extractor, 119
Bittle, Jake, 2, 34
Boehm, Jessica, 102
boiler, 95

| 137

138 | INDEX

bomb threats
    library preparedness/response to, 51–52
    as man-made disasters, 47
    procedures for library, 100–101
born-digital collections, 114
Boston Marathon bombings, 51
Brewer, Michelle Volesko, 9
Brobst, John L., 10
Broekhuizen, Kim, 101
Brown, Michael, 53
building information models, 112
buildings
    Chugiak-Eagle River Library after earthquake, 76–79
    facility maintenance/preparations, 93–94
    fire at Harvest Park Middle School, 81–85
    flooding of Dow Memorial Library, 86–90
    inspections of, 94–98
    physical security of library, 104–108
    See also physical facilities
bulk extractor, Bitcurator, 119
Bureau of Public Roads, 2
Burton Barr Central Library, Phoenix, Arizona, 102
Bush, George W., 4

C

California Department of Forestry and Fire Protection, 80
California State Library, 9
Camp Fire, 80
Canada, 107–108
Carnes, Sarah, 8
Carter, Jimmy, ix, 3
Centers for Disease Control and Prevention (CDC)
    disaster planning resources of, 18–19
    on earthquake preparedness, 75
    "Take Action" digital media toolkit, 22
    trauma-informed approach training, 46
chain of custody, 115
Chancellor, Renate, 53
Chemical Hazards Emergency Medical Management (CHEMM) tool, 21–22
children
    comforting, 43
    evacuation procedures and, 99, 100
    helping children cope with disaster, 46
    library disaster plan and, 90
Chugiak-Eagle River Library, Anchorage, Alaska, 75–79
civil defense, 2

civil unrest
    library response to, 52–54
    as man-made disaster, 47
Clark, Nancy, 77, 78
Clifton, Shari, 30–31
climate change
    fire season and, 80
    as great threat, ix
    hurricane preparedness and, 65
    library hosting of climate change discussions, 128
    See also global warming
cloud storage, 117
Cold War era, 2
collections
    analog collections, 111–114
    cleaning/salvaging artifacts after disaster, 44–45
    digital collections, 114–119
    fire at Harvest Park Middle School, 81–83
    flooding of Port Arthur Public Library, 66–69
    tornadoes, damage from, 71–73
    See also library materials
comfort, 43–44
communication
    about fire at Harvest Park Middle School, 82
    about flooding of library, 89
    at APTrust, 117
    communications plan for tornadoes, 70
    in disaster plan, 79
    in evacuation procedures, 99
    for library emergency response exercise, 59
    literacy concerns in disaster preparedness, 122–124
community
    Chugiak-Eagle River Library after earthquake and, 77–78
    civil unrest, 52–54
    comfort, promoting, 43–44
    COVID-19 pandemic/information access, 55–57
    disaster response by libraries and, 10
    disaster response phases, 40–41
    engagement in disaster preparedness, 48
    human element of disaster preparedness/response, 39–40
    hurricanes and, 65
    individual responses to disaster response/recovery, 41–43

input on rebuilding process, 45
libraries as cornerstone of community function, 124
libraries in community disaster management, 121–122
library disaster preparedness and, 128–129
literacy concerns in disaster preparedness, 122–124
relationships for disaster preparedness, 26–27
community agencies, 20, 123
community assessment projects, 123
community planning department, 19
confidentiality, 119
conservation assistance, 119
consortia
    Academic Preservation Trust, 116–118
    for digital preservation, 115
contact information, 113
contacts document, 89
coronavirus pandemic
    See COVID-19 pandemic
Corrigan, Andy, 6
Cottrell, Megan, 53
Council of State Archivists (CoSA), 20–21
COVID-19 pandemic
    coping mechanisms for, 41–42
    disaster preparedness games and, 33–34
    Grace A. Dow Memorial Library and, 86, 89
    Haskell Free Library & Opera House and, 108
    human element of, 54–58
    information access in Latinx community and, 55–57
    as interconnectedness reminder, 1
    internet access at library during, x
    Jaffrey Public Library's doll hospital, 128
    Lawrence County Public Library and, 72
    learning opportunities from, xi
    librarians and, ix
    library responses to, 54–55
    literacy concerns/information resources, 122
    social/health inequities and, 47
COVID-19 Recovery site (ALA), 55
CREST (Cultural Resource Emergency Support Team), 44–45
Cristy, Page, 41–42
cultural heritage institutions
    in Academic Preservation Trust, 116, 117–118

archives analog collections, 114
disaster planning consultation/training, 9–10
Cultural Resource Emergency Support Team (CREST), 44–45
culture, 1
cybersecurity attacks, 32

D

Daigle, Bradley, 116–118
dams, 86–87
dark archive, 118–119
Davis, Adam S., 124
Daytime Emergency Evacuation Procedures, 99–100
Dearborn, Carly, 117
designated meeting place, 99
development, 64–65
Dewan, Shaila K., xi
Diamond, Andrew, 118
Diamond, Tom, 7
digital collections
    Academic Preservation Trust, 116–118
    chain of custody in disaster recovery process, 115
    distributed storage, 115, 118
    fragility of, 115
    levels of access, 118–119
    terms for, 114
digital preservation consortia
    Academic Preservation Trust, 116–118
    for digital preservation, 115
digital resources, 10
digitized collections, 114
Direct Relief International, 11
disaster, ix
disaster declarations
    federal disaster declarations, 7
    FEMA building damage disaster declarations, 104–105
    flooding FEMA disaster declarations, 86
Disaster Information Management Research Center (DIMRC)
    disaster planning resources of, 8–9, 18
    mobile applications for disaster management, 21–22
    sample social media policy, 23–24
Disaster Information Management Resource Center, ix
Disaster Information Specialization program, 27, 126

INDEX

disaster management
  for analog collections, 111–114
  for digital collections, 114–119
  libraries in community disaster management, 121–122
  See also emergency management
disaster plan
  for analog collections, 111–114
  of APTrust, 116–118
  bomb threat procedures, 100–101
  for earthquakes, 78–79
  evacuation procedures, 99–100
  fire plan, 98
  for flooding, 89–90
  importance of, 128–129
  individual responses to disasters and, 41
  library disaster plan, elements of, 16–17
  pest management, 101
  for physical facilities, 101–102
  physical facilities, information related to, 97–98
  of Pleasanton Unified School District, 84
  of Port Arthur Public Library, 68–69
  salvage procedures in, 102–103
  sharing, 102
  for tornadoes, 73
  on vandalism, 102
disaster planning
  "Disaster Planning for Libraries" class, 15–16
  earthquake planning, resources for, 79–80
  final thoughts on, 128–129
  fire planning, resources for, 85
  flood planning, resources for, 90–91
  hurricane planning, resources for, 69
  by libraries, recent history of, 6–8
  libraries and, 8–10
  library disaster plan, elements of, 16–17
  tools, 17–21
  tornado planning, resources for, 73–74
"Disaster Planning for Libraries" class, 15–16
disaster planning tools
  community/nonprofit agencies, 20
  federal agencies, 17–19
  libraries with experience of disasters, 20
  service continuity plan, 20–21
  state/local governments and agencies, 19–20
"Disaster Preparation and Recovery" (MedlinePlus), 18
disaster preparedness
  disaster plan, elements of, 16–17
  disaster planning tools, 17–21
  disaster plans, libraries with, 15–16
  games, disaster-related, 33–34
  go-bag, items for, 28–30
  hurricane planning, resources for, 69
  mitigation, 34–36
  physical facilities, maintenance of, 93
  relationships for, 26–27
  risk assessment, 30–32
  technologies for disaster management, 21–26
  training with emergency responders, 27–28
"Disaster Preparedness and Emergency Response" course (Emporia State University), 125
disaster preparedness and response
  building inspections for, 94–98
  disaster response, phases of, 40–41
  final thoughts on, 128
  human element of, 39–40
  librarians as trained disaster response specialists, 124–126
  literacy concerns in, 122–124
  response by libraries, support of general public, 10
disaster recovery plan, of APTrust, 116–118
disaster relief, 1–6
Disaster Relief Act of 1974, 7
"Disaster Response and Continuity of Operations Procedures" (Environmental Protection Agency Library), 9
disaster supplies
  go bag, items for, 28–30
  interior building inspection assessment, 95
  library stockpile of, 113–114
Disaster Technical Assistance Center (DTAC), 40–41
disasters
  disaster planning by libraries, recent history of, 6–8
  federal government's role in disaster relief, 1–6
  human element of, 39–40
  interconnectedness of society, environment, culture, 1
  library services during, ix
  man-made disasters, 46–48
disillusionment phase, 40
disinformation, 55–57

INDEX | 141

distributed storage
    Academic Preservation Trust, 116–118
    for digital special collections, 115, 118
Doak, Cecilia C., 56
documentation, 119
domestic violence, 47–48
Donahue, Amy, 124
Do's and Don'ts, for disaster response, 42
drills
    for evacuation procedures, 99
    for library workers, 128
    for physical safety of library workers/
        users, 106
    for tornadoes, 70
drugs, 49–50
DTAC (Disaster Technical Assistance Center), 40–41
Duke University, 24–26
Dunkin, Ann, 9

E

Earthquake Country Alliance, 32, 80
"Earthquake Hazards Prepare" (USGS), 79
earthquakes
    adverse effects after, 47–48
    field report from Chugiak-Eagle River Library, 75–79
    overview of, 74–75
    resources for earthquake planning, 79–80
    risks of by regions, 63
Edwards, Christian, 44–45
electrical cords, 95
electrician, 94
emergency alerts, 21
emergency management
    federal government's role in, 1–6
    by libraries, recent history of, 6–8
    See also disaster management
Emergency Management Institute (FEMA), 27
emergency necessities
    See disaster supplies
"Emergency Preparedness" (CDC), 18–19
Emergency Preparedness Committee, 58–60
emergency responders
    library Emergency Preparedness Committee and, 58
    library relationships with, 8
    for patron exhibiting threatening behavior, 106–107
    relationships with, 8, 27
    training with, 27–28

See also first responders
Emporia State University, 125
environment, 1
    See also climate change
environmental hazards, 106
Environmental Protection Agency Library, 9
"essential community function," 7
evacuation
    of patrons from library, 90
    procedures, 99–100
    warning for flooding, 86–87
exterior building inspection assessment, 97

F

facility team, 93
FAIC (Foundation for Advancement in Conservation), 9, 114
Featherstone, Robin M., 124
federal agencies, 17–19
Federal Civil Defense Administration (FCDA), 2
Federal Emergency Management Agency (FEMA)
    broad mandate of, 6
    building safety evaluations after disaster, 105–106
    at Chugiak-Eagle River Library, 77, 79
    on civil unrest, 52
    disaster declarations related to building damage, 104–105
    disaster mitigation for Sidney Memorial Public Library, 35–36
    disaster mitigation grants, 34
    disaster planning resources of, 18
    disaster preparedness games, resources for, 33
    establishment of, 3
    on Flood Control Act, 2
    flooding, definition of, 85
    flooding as cause of building damage, 86
    funding for Port Arthur Public Library, 68
    Hurricane Katrina, response to, 4–5
    libraries' disaster planning/response and, 6–8
    Oklahoma City bombing, 4
    resources for flood planning, 91
    response capability of, 3–4
    risk assessment resources, 31–32
    on safe room for tornadoes, 70
    training opportunities, 27

federal government
   libraries' disaster planning/response and, 6-8
   role in disaster relief, 1-6
FEMA
   See Federal Emergency Management Agency
Ferguson Municipal Public Library, 53
Ferraro, Paul, 65
field report
   from Chugiak-Eagle River Library after earthquake, 75-79
   from Grace A. Dow Memorial Library about flooding, 86-90
   from Harvest Park Middle School about fire, 81-85
   introduction to, 63-64
   from Lawrence County Public Library about tornado, 70-73
   from Port Arthur Public Library about Hurricane Harvey, 65-69
file formats, 115
fire department
   for disaster preparedness help, 19-20
   in fire plan, 98
   library disaster plan, sharing with, 102
fire drills, 95
fire extinguishers
   checks of, 20, 28
   in fire plan, 98
   interior building inspection assessment, 96
   interior building inspection schedule, 95
   in library's disaster plan, 97
fire plan, 98
fires
   arson, 52
   field report from Harvest Park Middle School, 81-85
   at JFK Presidential Library, 51-52
   library preparedness for, 80-81
   overview of, 80
   resources for fire planning, 85
first responders
   building safety evaluations after disaster, 106
   map of valuable items in archives for, 112
   relationships with, 27, 113
   tips for working with people after disaster, 42-43
   See also emergency responders

Flaherty, Mary Grace
   library building issues handled by, 103-104
   paying it forward, 127
Flood Control Act, 2
Flood Insurance Act of 1968, 2
Flood Inundation Mapper, 90
flooding
   of Burton Barr Central Library, 102
   of Grace A. Dow Memorial Library, 86-90
   hurricane planning, resources for, 69
   from hurricanes, 64
   overview of, 85-86
   of Port Arthur Public Library, 66-69
   resources for flood planning, 90-91
   shelving units and, 112
   of Sidney Memorial Public Library, 35-36
floods, 85-91
Florida Division of Emergency Management, 69
Florido, Adrian, 48
Floyd, George, 53
Ford, Anne, 49
Forry, Bill, 51
Foundation for Advancement in Conservation (FAIC), 114
Fountain, Henry, 63
fragility, of digital collections, 115
Franklin, Benjamin, 15
Freedom House, ix
Fuchs, Matthew, 34
funding
   for disaster mitigation, 34-36
   for Port Arthur Public Library's recovery/ rebuilding, 68
   for reformatting, 115
   Stafford Act on, 7
furnace cleaning, 95
future opportunities
   final thoughts on disaster preparedness, 128-129
   librarian as trained disaster response specialists, 124-126
   libraries in community disaster management, 121-122
   literacy concerns in disaster preparedness/response, 122-124
   paying it forward, 127
   support, library's role of, 121

G

games, disaster-related, 33-34
Gaul, Gilbert M.

on cost of rebuilding after hurricanes, 65
Geography of Risk: Epic Storms, Rising Seas, and the Cost of America's Coasts, 69
on hurricanes, 64
on spending on climate-related disasters, 63
generator, 19
Geography of Risk: Epic Storms, Rising Seas, and the Cost of America's Coasts (Gaul), 69
The Global 2000 Report to the President (Barney), ix
global warming
    flooding risks and, 86
    weather-related disasters due to, 63
    See also climate change
go-bag, 28–30
Gonzalez, Davila, 8
government
    See federal government; local government; state government
Grace, Cathy, 46
Grace A. Dow Memorial Library, Midland, Michigan, 86–90
grants, 34
Gray, Freddie, 53
Great Alaska earthquake, 76
Greene, Katherine, 64

H

Haitian Creole materials, 123
Halsted, Deborah D., 30–31
Harvest Park Middle School, Pleasanton, California, 81–85
Haskell Free Library & Opera House, 107–108
Hayslett, Michele, 58–60
HAZUS program (FEMA), 32
health care services, 55–57
HealthReach, 57
Healthy Heart Hospital (board game), 34
Hennepin County East Lake Library, 53
Heritage Emergency and Response Training (HEART), 10
Heritage Emergency National Task Force, 9–10
heroic phase, 40
high-density storage, 24–26
Homeland Security Act, 4
honeymoon phase, 40
The Hub, 128
Hughes, Kathleen, 54
human element
    active shooters, 50–51

    arson, 52
    bomb threats, 51–52
    civil unrest, 52–54
    community engagement, 48
    COVID-19 pandemic, 54–58
    of disaster preparedness, response, and recovery, 39–40
    disaster response phases, 40–41
    individual responses, 41–43
    man-made disasters, 46–48
    opportunities, seizing, 58–60
    other duties of libraries, 49–50
    support, offering, 43–46
    volunteers, 48–49
Hunt, Kyla, 19
Hurricane Florence, 44–45
Hurricane Harvey, 65–69
Hurricane Katrina
    federal government's response to, 4–5
    libraries' disaster plans/response to, 6–7
    libraries helping other libraries after, 127
    physical victimization of women after, 47
Hurricane Laura, 19
Hurricane Maria, 8, 48
hurricanes
    field report from Port Arthur Public Library, 66–69
    library preparedness for, 65
    overview of, 64–65
    resources for hurricane planning, 69
    risks of by regions, 63
HVAC systems, 88, 103–104

I

Illinois Fire Service Institute Library, 85
impact phase, 40
Indian Education Resource Center at the University of North Carolina at Pembroke, 44–45
individual responses, 41–43
Indonesia, 47–48
Infection: Humanity's Last Grasp (board game), 34
infographics, 122
information
    access to, COVID-19 pandemic and, 55–57
    library as information provider for community, 121–122
    literacy concerns in disaster preparedness, 122–124
information literacy, 22
Inklebarger, Timothy, 53

inspections
- exterior building inspection assessment, 97
- interior building inspection assessment, 96
- interior building inspection schedule, 95
- of library facilities, routine, 93
- of library facility after disaster, 104–105
- of physical facilities, 94–98

Institute of Museum and Library Services, 54

insurance
- for flooding, 86
- library disaster plan, sharing with insurance carrier, 102
- library internet access for filing insurance claims, 10
- policies for physical facilities, 94–95
- in risk assessment process, 31

insurance agent, 94
interior building inspection assessment, 96
interior building inspection schedule, 95
international agencies, 10–11
International Committee of the Red Cross, 11
International Conference on Massive Storage Systems and Technology, 116
International Federation of the Red Cross, 11

internet access
- COVID-19 pandemic/information access in Latinx community, 56, 57
- at Lawrence County Public Library after tornado, 72
- library services after disaster, 10
- technologies for disaster management and, 21

inventory
- of library for tornado recovery, 73
- of library holdings for hurricane preparedness, 68

IT department, 128–129

J

Jaffrey Public Library, 128
Jankow, Chris, 124
John F. Kennedy (JFK) Presidential Library and Museum, 51–52
Johnson, Earl
- on Noah's ark, ix
- on ways to comfort, 43–44

JUNTOS Radio: Salud Sin Filtros (podcast), 57

K

Kennedy, John F., 2

King, Susan, 82

L

LaFaro, Alyssa, 48, 64
Landgraf, Greg, 32
language
- COVID-19 Spanish-language resources, 57
- of disaster information resources, 122, 123
- information access in Latinx community and, 55–57

Latinx community, 55–57
Law, Vernon, 1
Lawrence County Public Library, Tennessee, 70–73
Lawrenceburg, Tennessee, 70–73
leak, 103–104
legislation, for disaster management, 1–6

librarians
- Christian Edwards on disaster response, 44–45
- comfort, promoting, 43–44
- disaster recovery support, 10
- individual responses to disasters, 41–43
- literacy concerns in disaster preparedness, 122–124
- Stafford Act amendment, work for, 7
- as trained disaster response specialists, 124–126
- *See also* library workers

The Librarian's Disaster Planning and Community Resiliency Guidebook (New Jersey State Library), 10

libraries
- active shooter events, response to, 50–51
- arson, prevention of, 52
- bomb threats and, 51–52
- building inspections, 94–98
- caretaking of facilities, x–xi
- civil unrest, response to, 52–54
- comfort, promoting, 43–44
- in community disaster management, 121–122
- community engagement of, 48
- COVID-19 pandemic, responses to, 54–55
- disaster planning, intersection of, 8–10
- disaster planning, recent history of, 6–8
- disaster planning tools, 17–21
- with disaster plans, 15–16
- disaster preparedness, final thoughts on, 128–129
- disaster recovery and response, x

disaster response/support of general public, 10
Emergency Preparedness Committee, 58–60
experienced with disasters, as resource, 20
federal government's role in disaster relief and, 6
field report from Chugiak-Eagle River Library after earthquake, 75–79
field report from Port Arthur Public Library about Hurricane Harvey, 66–69
fire planning, resources for, 85
fires, field report from Harvest Park Middle School, 81–85
fires, preparedness for, 80–81
human element of disaster preparedness/response and, 39–40
hurricanes, preparedness/recovery, 64–69
individual responses to disasters and, 41–43
librarians as trained disaster response specialists, 124–126
library as cornerstone of community function, 124
library disaster plan, elements of, 16–17
literacy concerns in disaster preparedness, 122–124
mitigation for disaster preparedness, 34–36
as not essential services in disaster response, 4, 5
opioid epidemic, response to, 49–50
physical security of, 104–108
preparedness, go-bag, 28–30
preparedness, relationships for, 26–27
preparedness, training for, 27–28
risk assessment for disaster planning, 30–32
technologies for disaster management, 21–26
tornadoes, preparation for/recovery from, 70–74
volunteers, plan for, 48–49
See also physical facilities
library and information science (LIS) programs, 125
Library Journal, 51
library materials
analog collections, 111–114
cleaning/salvaging after disaster, 44–45
cleanup after library fire, 81–83

COVID-19 virus, surface transmission, 54
digital collections, 114–119
flooding of Dow Memorial Library, 87–88
flooding of Port Arthur Public Library, 66–69
salvage procedures, 102–103
tornadoes, damage from, 71–73
See also collections
library patrons
active shooters and, 50, 51
of Chugiak-Eagle River Branch Library, 77–78
evacuation procedures and, 99–100
of Grace A. Dow Memorial Library, 89
in library disaster plan, 90
library help for after disaster, 10
physical safety of, 106, 107
tornadoes and, 71
Library Service Center (LSC) of Duke University, 24–26
"Library Staff as Public Servants: A Field Guide for Preparing to Support Communities in Crisis" (Subramaniam), 45–46
library workers
active shooter events, response to, 50–51
arson, response to, 52
bomb threat procedures, 100–101
bomb threats and, 51–52
civil unrest, response to, 52–54
cleaning/salvaging artifacts after disaster, 45–46
COVID-19 pandemic, responses to, 54–55
disaster preparedness, engagement in, 128, 129
disaster response after Hurricane Florence, 44–45
evacuation procedures, 99–100
field report from Chugiak-Eagle River Library, 75–79
field report from Lawrence County Public Library, 70–73
field report from Port Arthur Public Library, 66–69
flooding of Grace A. Dow Memorial Library and, 86–90
individual responses to disasters, 41–43
opioid epidemic, response to, 49–50
physical safety of, 106
volunteers, plan for, 48–49
See also librarians
Lightbody, Laura, 34

Linares, Brenda, 55–57
Lions Club International, 20
literacy concerns, 122–124
local government
    building safety evaluations after disaster, 106
    disaster preparedness resources of, 19–20
    disaster response by, 3
    relationship with, 113
    risk assessment team and, 31
LOCKSS (Lots of Copies Keep Stuff Safe), 116
Los Angeles County Sheriff's Office, 50
Los Angeles Public Library, 52
Lynch, Deborah, 9

M

mainshocks, 74
maintenance
    for disaster preparedness, 128
    of physical facilities, 93–94
management, 117
    See also disaster management
Mandel, Lauren H., 10
man-made disasters
    active shooters, 50–51
    arson, 52
    bomb threats, 51–52
    civil unrest, 52–54
    overview of, 46–48
maps, of collections, 112, 113
markings, 112, 113
master list, 112
mayor's office, 19
McClure, Charles R., 10
McKay, Jim, 10
McMahon, Jeff, 22
Medecins sans Frontieres (Doctors without Borders), 11
Medical Library Association (MLA), 27, 126
Mediterranean recluse spiders, 101
MedlinePlus, 18
Meister, Sam, 117
Meltzer-Brody, Samantha, 41–42
Memoranda of Understanding (MOUs)
    function of, 9
    Model Memorandum of Understanding, 131–136
Mener, Andrew S., 3, 4
Michigan National Guard, 88
Midland, Michigan, 86–90
Minneapolis Central Library, 53

misinformation
    bomb threats and, 51–52
    COVID-19 pandemic/information access in Latinx community, 55–57
    library as information provider for community, 121
    from social media, 22
Miskel, James F., 3
"mission creep," 49–50
mitigation
    archives disaster management for, 112–114
    building inspections for, 94–98
    for disaster preparedness, 34–36
    from FEMA/from nonprofit agencies, 34
    flooding at Sidney Memorial Public Library, 35–36
    physical facilities, maintenance of, 93
    in risk assessment process, 31
    savings from, 34
MLA (Medical Library Association), 27, 126
mobile applications, 21–22
Model Memorandum of Understanding, 9, 131–136
Modified Mercalli Scale (MMS), 74
More Powerful NC, 49
MOUs
    See Memoranda of Understanding
Mt. Saint Helens Volcano (board game), 34

N

naloxone, 49
National Center for Preservation Technology and Training, 34
National Child Traumatic Stress Network, 74
National Council of State Housing Agencies, 91
National Endowment for the Humanities, 34
National Flood Insurance Program, 2, 86
National Governors Association, 3
National Guard, 3
National Heritage Responders, 9, 114
National Historical Publications and Records Commission grants, 34
National Hurricane Center, 69
National Intelligence Council, ix
National Interagency Fire Center, 85
National Library of Medicine (NLM)
    on amended Stafford Act, 7
    DIMRC, 18
    Disaster Information Specialization program, 126
    as disaster planning resource, 8–9

disaster preparedness games, resources for, 33
MedlinePlus, disaster planning tools, 18
mobile applications for disaster management, 21–22
Model Memorandum of Understanding, 131–136
on role of libraries in disaster response/recovery, 5
National Network of Libraries of Medicine (NNLM)
   Model Memorandum of Understanding, 9
   Pacific Southwest Region COVID-19 Spanish-Language Resources, 57
   relationships with local emergency responders, 8
National Oceanic and Atmospheric Administration (NOAA)
   disaster preparedness games, resources for, 33
   hurricane planning, resources of, 69
   Saffir-Simpson Hurricane Wind Scale, 64
National Preparedness month, 129
National Weather Service
   flood planning resources of, 91
   hurricane planning resources of, 69
   on preparedness for tornadoes, 70
   tornado planning resources of, 73
   on weather-related disasters, x
natural disasters
   adverse effects after, 47–48
   earthquakes, 74–80
   federal government's role in disaster relief, 1–6
   fires, 80–85
   floods, 85–91
   hurricanes, 64–69
   increase in, 63
   librarian experiences in dealing with, x
   tornadoes, 70–74
NEDCC (Northeast Document Conservation Center), 102, 113–114
New England Historical Society, 2
New Jersey State Library, 10, 103
New Orleans, Louisiana, 6–7
New Zealand, 47
Newton, Teresa, 70–73
NLM
   See National Library of Medicine
NNLM
   See National Network of Libraries of Medicine

NOAA
   See National Oceanic and Atmospheric Administration
Noack, Rick, 33
nongovernmental organizations, 3
nonprofit agencies, 20, 34
North Carolina, 49
North Carolina Department of Natural and Cultural Resources, 44
North Carolina Library Association, 46
Northeast Document Conservation Center (NEDCC), 102, 113–114

O

OCLC, 54
Office of Civil and Defense Mobilization, 2
Office of Defense Mobilization, 2
Office of Emergency Planning, 2
Office of National Preparedness, 4
Office of Public Health Preparedness and Response, 46
Ohio State University, 50–51
Oklahoma City bombing, 4
Oliver-Smith, Anthony, 1
Olson, Rochelle, 53
opioid epidemic, 49–50
opportunities, seizing, 58–60
Orlean, Susan, 52
Ozbay, Fatih, 121

P

Pandemic (board game), 34
Pandemic: The Cure (board game), 34
Paradise, California, 80
Parkinson, Debra, 47
Pass Christian, Mississippi, 127
patrons
   See library patrons
paying it forward, 127
pest management, 101
Petrelli, Stefano, 33
Pham-Bui, Trang, 127
physical facilities
   bomb threat procedures, 100–101
   disaster plan, other considerations, 101–102
   evacuation procedures, 99–100
   fire plan, 98
   inspections of, 94–98
   maintenance/preparations related to disaster planning, 93–94
   minor/major building issues, 103–104

148 | INDEX

physical facilities *(continued)*
  physical security, 104–108
  salvage priorities/procedures, 102–103
  See also buildings; libraries
physical security, 104–108
Pivoting during the Pandemic: Ideas for Serving Your Community Anytime, Anywhere (Hughes & Santoro), 54
Plague (board game), 34
plan
  See disaster plan
Pleasanton, California, 81–85
Pleasanton Unified School District, 82, 83–84
Pocket Response Plan (PReP), 20–21
police department
  in bomb threat procedures, 100–101
  for disaster preparedness help, 19
  library disaster plan, sharing with, 102
  in Pass Christian library during hurricane, 127
  protests over killings by police, 53
policy, social media, 23–24
Port Arthur Public Library, Texas, 65–69
Post-Disaster Building Safety Evaluation Guidance (FEMA), 104
pre-disaster phase, 40
Preservation Technology and Training Grants, 34
president, U.S.
  federal disaster declarations by, 7
  FEMA disaster relief and, 3
protests, 52–54
psychological reactions
  to disasters, 40–41
  individual responses to disasters, 41–43
public libraries, 15–16
Public Library Association, 46
Puerto Rico, 8, 48

Q
Quinlan, Hannah, 101

R
RACE, 100
Radiation Emergency Medical Management (REMM), 22
rainfall
  flooding at Grace A. Dow Memorial Library, 86
  from Hurricane Harvey, 66
  with hurricanes, 64–65
  with tornadoes, 71

ransomware attacks, 129
rare materials, 119
readability checkers, 122–123
Ready.gov (FEMA)
  disaster planning resources on, 18
  disaster preparedness games, resources for, 33
  for risk assessment resources, 31–32
REALM (REopening Archives, Libraries, and Museums) project, 54
Reconstruction Finance Corporation, 2
reconstruction phase, 40–41
records
  chain of custody for digital archival materials, 115
  of costs/activities for disaster reimbursement, 6
recovery
  of Chugiak-Eagle River Library after earthquake, 76–79
  of Grace A. Dow Memorial Library after flooding, 88–90
  of Harvest Park Middle School after fire, 81–85
  of Lawrence County Public Library after tornado, 71–73
  of Port Arthur Public Library after Hurricane Harvey, 66–69
  of rare materials, 119
  See also disaster preparedness and response
red building designation, 104
Reed, Jack, 7
REFORMA, 8
reformatting, 115
Reich, Barbara S., 9
reimbursement process, 6
relationships
  for disaster preparedness, 26–27
  disaster response phases and, 40
REMM (Radiation Emergency Medical Management), 22
REopening Archives, Libraries, and Museums (REALM) project, 54
resources
  for active shooter events training, 50–51
  for archives disaster management, 114
  COVID-19 Spanish-language resources, 57
  disaster planning tools, 17–21
  for disaster preparedness games, 33–34
  for earthquake planning, 79–80
  for fire planning, 85

for flood planning, 90–91
for hurricane planning, 69
for risk assessment, 31–32
on salvage procedures, 102–103
for tornado planning, 73–74
for weather-related disasters, 64
Richter Scale, 74–75
riots, 52–54
risk assessment
in disaster planning process, xi
for disaster preparedness, 30–32
for hurricane planning, 69
of library for natural disasters, 91
steps for conducting, 30–32
"Risks to Digital Information" (LOCKSS workshop), 116
Robert T. Stafford Disaster Relief and Emergency Assistance Act, 7
Rossen, L. M., 122
Rotary International, 20
Rubenstein Library of Duke University, 25
Ruffner, Flavia, 116–118
Rumery, Nancy, 108
Runyon, Michelle, 116–118
Rural Women's Health Project, 57

S

safe room, 70
Saffir-Simpson Hurricane Wind Scale, 64
salvage, 102–103
Salvation Army, 3, 11
San Jose State University, 125
sanitation department, 19
Santoro, Jamie, 54
Savidge, Martin, 127
Schneider, Saundra K., 3
school libraries, 16
Schumacher, Julie A., 47
SCPL (Spartanburg County Public Library), 32
security, physical, 104–108
Sendaula, Stephanie, 51
service continuity plan, 20–21
service disruption, 118
ServPro restoration experts, 71–73, 88–89
Sesame Street, 33
shelving units, 112
shootings
active shooters, library response to, 50–51
as man-made disasters, 47
Shores, Elizabeth, 46

Sidney Memorial Public Library, Sidney, New York, 127
smartphones, 21–22
Smith, Monica, 34
smoke damage, 81–83
smoke detectors, 95
social media
COVID-19 pandemic/information access in Latinx community, 56
for disaster management, 22–23
social media policy, sample of, 23–24
social support, 121
society, 1
Society of American Archivists, 9
Spanish language, 55–57
Spartanburg County Public Library (SCPL), 32
special collections
See archives and special collections
Stafford Act of 2011, 34
state government
disaster preparedness resources of, 19–20
disaster response by, 3
federal disaster declaration, request for, 7
state governors
federal disaster declaration, request for, 7
request for disaster relief from, 3
state libraries, 16
storage
distributed storage, 115–118
high-density storage, 24–26
strengths/weaknesses, 31
stress, 90
structural accidents, 102
structural damage, 104
Subramaniam, Mega, 45–46
support, 43–46
surface transmission, of viruses, 54
"Surviving an Active Shooter" (Los Angeles County Sheriff's Office), 50
Sustaining Cultural Heritage Collections grant, 34
SWOT matrix, 31
Syrus, Publilius, 36

T

"Take Action" digital media toolkit (CDC), 22
team, 30–31
technological security challenges, xi
technologies
for disaster management, 21–26
emergency alerts, 21

high-density storage, 24–26
mobile applications, 21–22
social media, 22–24
tracking technologies, 22
templates
  exterior building inspection assessment, 97
  interior building inspection assessment, 96
  interior building inspection schedule, 95
Tennessee Valley Authority, 2
terrorism, 4–5
Texas, 65–69
Texas State Library, 19
thanks, 49
Three Mile Island nuclear plant, 3
timeline, of federal involvement in disaster relief, 5
Tobin, Tess, 8
Tolley, Rebecca, 46
"Tools for Practitioners" (ready.gov), 18
Topper, Elisa F., 6–7
tornadoes
  field report from Lawrence County Public Library, Tennessee, 70–73
  overview of, 70
  resources for tornado planning, 73–74
  risks of, 63
tracking technologies, 22
training
  for active shooter events response, 50–51
  for civil unrest, response to, 53–54
  with emergency responders, 27–28
  for fire preparedness, 98
  by HEART, 10
  librarians as trained disaster response specialists, 124–126
  library emergency response exercise, 58–60
  for mobile applications, 22
  on trauma-informed approach, 46
transparency, 116–117
A Trauma-Informed Approach to Library Services (Tolley), 46
trauma-informed service, 46
Trusted Digital Repository certification process, 116, 118
tsunami, 47–48
Tulane University Howard-Tilton Memorial Library, 6–7

U

UN Office for Disaster Risk Reduction, 33
UNDRR (UN Office for Disaster Risk Reduction), 11
UNEP (UN Environmental Programme Disasters and Conflicts sub-programme), 11
UNHCR (UN High Commissioner for Refugees), 11
UNICEF (UN Children's Fund), 11
United Nations (UN) agencies, 10–11
United States, 107–108
University of Michigan, 101
University of North Carolina at Chapel Hill
  disaster preparedness course, 125
  School of Information & Library Science, 15–16
  School of Medicine, 41–42
  UNC at Chapel Hill Libraries, 58–60
University of North Texas, 125
University of Virginia
  Academic Preservation Trust, 116–118
  Disaster Information Specialization program, 126
UN-Water, 11
U.S. Army Corps of Engineers, 2
U.S. Department of Health and Human Services
  DTAC on phases of disaster response, 40–41
  tips for working with people after disaster, 43
U.S. Department of Homeland Security
  on active shooter events, 51
  creation of/response to disasters, 4–5
  physical security of Haskell Free Library & Opera House, 107–108
U.S. Geological Survey (USGS)
  Flood Inundation Mapper, 90
  Modified Mercalli Scale, use of, 74
  resources for earthquake planning, 79
usability, 115
utility personnel, 106

V

vaccines, 56–57
vandalism, 102
Vardell, Emily
  librarians as trained disaster response specialists, 124–126

literacy concerns in disaster preparedness, 122–124
virtual programming, 54
volunteers
    for disaster preparedness, response, recovery, 48–49
    disaster response after Hurricane Florence, 44–45
    in library emergency response exercise, 59
    plan for disaster recovery/response efforts, 48–49

W

war, xi
Washington Post, 33
weather-related disasters
    earthquakes, 74–80
    fires, 80–85
    floods, 85–91
    hurricanes, 64–69
    increase in, 63
    librarian experiences in dealing with, x
    tornadoes, 70–74
Whitmer, Gretchen, 86
Wi-Fi, 54
wildfires
    library preparedness for, 80–81
    overview of, 80
    resources for fire planning, 85
    risks of, 63
Williams, Steven, 65–69
Wilson, Daniel T., 30–31
winds
    hurricanes, 64–69
    from tornadoes, 70, 71
Wireless Information System for Emergency Responders (WISER), 21
Witt, James Lee, 4
women, 47–48
World Economic Forum, 85
World Health Organization (WHO), 11
Wrigley, Jordan, 49

Y

yellow building designation, 104

Z

Zara, Claire, 47

ALA TechSource

Learn more and subscribe at
alatechsource.org

Practical and concise, ALA TechSource publications help you

- Stay on top of emerging technologies
- Discover the latest tools proving effective in libraries
- Implement practical and time-saving strategies
- Learn from industry experts on topics such as privacy policies, online instruction, automation systems, digital preservation, artificial intelligence (AI), and more